The present ferment of excitement about Canadian literature has moved many of us to re-read our country's earlier poetry and fiction and welcome newer poets and novelists with a warmth that they could not have expected a generation ago. This scenebook attempts to promote a similar recognition for Canadian playwrights. In order to brief the traveller for his exploration of these scenes from our past and current theatre, Andrew Parkin has provided a concise survey of the entire terrain, and a brief introduction to each excerpt that he has chosen. As both Professor Parkin's remarks and the scenes themselves illustrate, Canadian drama provides an absorbing record of our past and present human concerns, and at its best makes powerful theatre.

John Stevens,
General Editor,
Festival Editions

D1684088

stage one

a canadian scenebook

Developed by Festival Editions

Edited by
Andrew Parkin
English Department,
University of British Columbia

General Editor
John Stevens
English Department,
Faculty of Education,
University of Toronto

Van Nostrand Reinhold Ltd., Toronto

New York, Cincinnati, London, Melbourne

Copyright © 1973 by Van Nostrand Reinhold Ltd., Toronto

All rights reserved. No part of this work covered by the copyrights hereon may be produced or used in any form or by any means - graphic, electronic, or mechanical, including photocopying, recording, taping, or information storage and retrieval systems - without the prior written permission of the publisher.

The use of the excerpts from the plays reprinted in this book is restricted to private reading and to theatre or dramatic arts students in the pursuit of their classroom studies. Presentation to the public of these excerpts, or any portions of them, in any form, is strictly forbidden unless prior permission has been obtained from the copyright holders.

ISBN 0 442 26452 6

Library of Congress Number 73-3777

Typography by Swift-o-type Limited

Printed and bound in Canada by The Bryant Press Limited

73 74 75 76 77 78   10 9 8 7 6 5 4 3 2 1

Acknowledgments

The author and publisher gratefully acknowledge those who have granted permission for the use of copyrighted material in this volume. Every reasonable care has been taken to credit copyright ownership correctly. The publisher would welcome information that will permit the correction of any errors or omissions in future printings.

A complete list of copyright owners will be found on page 174

Editor's Acknowledgement

I should here like to thank the authors and publishers who have permitted me to reprint examples of their work in this book. Help from the staff of U.B.C. Library has also been valuable to me, particularly so in the case of Sheila Neville, whose collection of Canadian play texts proved vital to my research. The encouragement and wisdom of John Stevens of the Faculty of Education, University of Toronto, and the constructive suggestions of Garry Lovatt of Van Nostrand Reinhold have been helpful in many ways. I have also been fortunate in having Don Stephens and Bill New as colleagues, and I am grateful to them for conversations which have been of help to me. Thanks finally are due to my wife, Christina, for her wit, alertness and goodsense.

Andrew Parkin,
University of British Columbia,
March, 1973.

Preface

Actors, like other people, learn best by doing. *Stage One* provides the student with a variety of excerpts from Canadian drama which offer widely differing challenges in acting and directing. This diversity is one big advantage of the scenebook over an anthology of full length plays, which by size is limited to a few plays, and which by cost is sometimes forced to avoid recent plays by living authors.

It is not my purpose to impose an acting method or "golden rules" in this anthology. That would be both undesirable and impossible. Every actor and teacher, and indeed, each excerpt will have a different set of potentialities. I have tried to provide scenes which call for a small number of people as well as those which call for crowd work to be practised. Each scene will demand work on such features of acting as conviction, empathy, imagination, the use of affective memory, rapport between characters, projection, physical and vocal control, the invention of precise and effective business, and the blocking out of movement. But the emphasis each scene should receive I leave to the discretion of those who use the book. They will be evolving rehearsal methods which suit their particular group and its circumstances. The reader searching for a specific kind of exercise, or interested in discovering more about the work of a given writer, may find useful the brief comments which precede every excerpt. It is here that details of the setting, time and general context of a scene and its characters are given.

Stage One is intended to provide a good idea of what is available in the way of interesting Canadian drama. It is not a substitute for complete plays, but an indication of the fast-growing range and mixture of quality in Canadian drama. Work on a brief scene will be barren indeed if the actors ignore the total play from which the morsel is taken. The skilful reader will go beyond the scene to the whole play, bringing back more ideas and feelings, fuller understanding of the characters, mood and tempo, more experience of the strengths and weaknesses of the writer, and more knowledge of Canadian plays. It is my hope that readers of this book will be stimulated to experience in full, not only the plays from which excerpts have been taken, but also some of the other works I have been unable to represent here. To this end, a select list of books for further reading is provided.

The drama class is by no means a mere fringe activity or a band wagon for the trendy; indeed, the practicalities of acting and basic staging procedures reveal numerous critical and interpretative problems often overlooked in textual studies. These problems clamour for solutions, sometimes on the spot, sometimes after concentrated thought and much trial and error; but they cannot be side-stepped. The drama class demands flexibility and inventiveness in both improvisation and careful rehearsal, in both spontaneity and meticulous exploration of a text and its implications. It presents an activity in which argument and discussion, cross-reference between disciplines, and sometimes important and necessary personal developments can occur. Situations that stimulate imagination, capacity for feeling, and critical thought; forms and styles that show some of the possibilities of drama as a dominant mode of expression in our time; language, conflicts and roles that reveal the connections between life at large and what is done in class; the capacity for building knowledge, self-confidence and the individual's sense of his appropriate place within the solidarity of the group—these are some of the crucial potentialities present in drama.

Stage One is the first scenebook to be devoted to Canadian drama. That such a venture, with this range of material, is now possible is, in itself, a clear indication that Canadian dramatists have lately been extraordinarily active. In Toronto alone, 1972 saw the production of over fifty Canadian plays. Only a few will survive, but a year which can boast two such powerful plays as David Freeman's *Creeps,* and David French's *Leaving Home,* has to be an especially significant date in the emergent history of drama in Canada.

Table of Contents

v Preface

viii Contents

ix Theatre and Drama in Canada: An Emerging Tradition

   Scenes from:
- 1 *La Guerre, Yes Sir!* by Roch Carrier
- 6 *The Killdeer* by James Reaney
- 12 *Nobody Waved Goodbye* by Don Owen
- 14 *The Labyrinth* by Charles Israel
- 18 *Charbonneau and Le Chef* by J. T. McDonough
- 28 *Goin' Down the Road* by William Fruet
- 31 *Fifteen Miles of Broken Glass* by Thomas Hendry
- 36 *Fortune and Men's Eyes* by John Herbert
- 39 *The Black Bonspiel of Wullie MacCrimmon* by W.O. Mitchell
- 43 *Do You Remember One September Afternoon?* by David Watmough
- 48 *Colours in the Dark* by James Reaney
- 54 *Leaving Home* by David French
- 60 *The Ecstasy of Rita Joe* by George Ryga
- 66 *Whiteoaks* by Mazo de la Roche
- 72 *Creeps* by David Freeman
- 76 *Branch Plant* by Harvey Markowitz
- 81 *Crabdance* by Beverley Simons
- 85 *He Didn't Even Say Goodbye* by Norman Williams
- 88 *Party Day* by Jack Winter
- 98 *Tecumseh* by Charles Mair
- 102 *Yesterday the Children Were Dancing* by Gratien Gélinas
- 111 *Overlaid* by Robertson Davies
- 121 *Riel* by John Coulter
- 127 *The Trial of Louis Riel* by John Coulter
- 131 *A Play on Words* by Lister Sinclair
- 137 *Does Anybody Here Know Denny?* by Sandy Stern
- 145 *Hunting Stuart* by Robertson Davies
- 152 *Burlap Bags* by Len Peterson
- 158 *Marsh Hay* by Merrill Denison

165 Chronological List of Contents

166 Scenes Classified According to Number and Sex of Characters

168 Canadian Theatre

169 Bibliography

174 Acknowledgements

Theatre and Drama in Canada: An Emerging Tradition

In Canada today there is a curious mixture of attitudes about Canadian culture. There is a demand for things Canadian, the continuing search for identity, the surge of nationalism, the cult of "this land", and mixed in with it all, modesty about the real achievements, together with dependence on foreign opinions. There is, too, a real lack of knowledge about Canadian drama. On the one hand, it would probably be true to say that there are many Canadian college graduates who, if asked to name four Canadian plays, could not do so; on the other hand, there is a growing interest in Canadian content. Many new plays are being written and produced, there are good theatres in the main urban areas, and there are many new theatre groups appearing.

A theatre, at its simplest, is an empty space in which there can be performance; it is the immediate environment of the actor, his gestures and the illusion which he creates. Theatres, as places of performance, exist in order to house the arts of the theatre. Theatre, in the broadest sense, occurs wherever people can be observed performing the vivid and exciting actions of human life. It makes its effects through sensations of all kinds, colour, movement, ritual and spectacle. It ranges from circus shows to pop concerts, and even to the organized battles of sport, as well as improvised and scripted plays.

Theatres can exist without dramatists. In nineteenth century England the drama was, in general, very poor from a literary point of view, yet theatrical activity at that time was extraordinarily intense. Ordinary people went by the thousands to see the melodramas of the day. Dramatists, however, need good performers and vigorous theatre if their plays are to come excitingly to life. Drama, as an art, thrives on conflict. It expresses through action, language and gesture the dynamics of being human. It is powered by the motives, desires, morality and words of its characters, reflecting the issues and struggles of their society. It is, then, a social art. It cannot flourish among small clusters of people scattered in rural isolation, but requires instead urban communities capable of providing some sort of theatre buildings and audiences.

In Canada most of the early theatres were built in the East. The earliest theatrical activity was in the Maritimes. In many communities amateur theatricals took place, the first recorded being Marc Lescarbot's masque, *Le Théâtre de Neptune* (1606). Performed partly in canoes and partly at a banquet at Port Royal, Acadia, it celebrated the arrival at the settlement of the nobleman, de Poutrincourt. He was feted with song, dance and the spectacle of Neptune, with six attendant Tritons, offering presents and speaking verses. Trumpets sounded, cannons fired, and then the procession made its way into the banqueting hall of the fortress. The entertainment, no doubt, helped to break the monotony and dispel some of the loneliness in the lives of the early settlers.

During the seventeenth and eighteenth centuries amateur groups performed in various settlements and garrisons. There is evidence of productions of Molière in Montreal. The first recorded theatre in Halifax was a production, on March 14, 1787, of Cumberland's *The West Indian*. Amateurs were still active there when Prince Edward came to the town in 1794. He saw their production of a play they called *The Mock Doctor*, probably based on Molière. American professional actors had worked in Halifax by 1816, and the practice of touring in Canada grew rapidly during the nineteenth century. The touring companies led to the building of theatres and the hiring of halls and other places which could be used as theatres. However, they also stunted and arrested the growth of Canadian amateur theatre in the last century. This dependency on outsiders meant that the need to foster local Canadian performers was forgotten in people's eagerness to see the American and British companies, which toured with entertainment ranging from variety turns and melodrama to works by Shakespeare.

The printing in 1776 at Montreal of Canada's first published play, *Jonathas et David*, by the French Jesuit, Père Pierre Brumoy (who never visited Canada), illustrates French dominance of the earliest beginnings of theatre and drama in Canada. Similarly, the building of Molson's Theatre Royal in 1825 in Montreal signifies a new era, that of the foreign English-speaking touring companies. Theatre Royal's first manager was an American; its first real star appearance was that of the Englishman, Edmund Kean, who played Richard III there in 1826. The Montreal public also saw Kean in *The Merchant of Venice, Othello* and *King Lear*. In 1833 Charles and Fanny Kemble were at the Theatre Royal, but judging by a letter Fanny wrote, the experience of touring in Canada was decidedly unpleasant in those days:

> "The heat while we were in Montreal was intolerable—the filth intolerable—the bugs intolerable—the people intolerable—the jargon they speak—intolerable. I lifted my hands in thankfulness when I again set foot in these United States."
>
> (Letter to Charles Matthews, Sr., 21. xii. 1834)

Another notable name which crops up in the history of theatrical Montreal is that of Charles Dickens. In 1842, during his first visit to America, Dickens went to Montreal, and there he appeared acting the parts of Gallop in *Deaf as a Post*, Alfred Highflyer in *A Roland for an Oliver*, and Mr. Snobington in *Two O'Clock in the Morning*. Before this first Theatre Royal closed down in 1845, it had another distinguished visitor. William Charles Macready, the English star actor, took a tour in America and visited Montreal in 1844, giving a performance of *Hamlet*.

Despite the rigours of touring in Canada, companies found that they could attract audiences and make money. During the nineteenth century, therefore, not only were theatres built, but three distinct touring circuits developed. The East, which included the Maritimes, Quebec and Ontario, stretching as far west as Winnipeg, was in effect part of the American New England circuit. Alberta and Saskatchewan afforded a touring route in the Middle West. British Columbia formed the northern part of a West Coast zone toured by companies from the American cities further down the coast. Then as now, the East was the main area for theatre and drama. The theatres were eventually owned almost entirely by American commercial managements, who brought in touring stock companies and various international stars. Despite the hypocritical habit of religious prudes in the nineteenth century of condemning theatres, performers and plays as wicked, this kind of prejudice did not prevent theatres from flourishing in Canada.

The dominance of foreign companies was probably the greatest single factor in stifling the growth of Canadian talent in theatre arts and playwriting. It is worth remembering, however, that there were some Canadian artists who appeared and managed to remain independent of the foreign companies for varying periods. By the year 1874, Charlotte Morrison had created her own stock company in Toronto. Their home was Toronto's Grand Opera House. "The Grand" opened with *The School for Scandal* in September 1874, in which Mrs. Morrison, as Lady Teazle, led her all-Canadian cast. Unfortunately, this local company folded five years later, when the theatre burned down. Another example of the beginnings of professional local acting is Harold Nelson's Canadian Dramatic Company, which worked the Walker theatrical circuit that took in the Red River Valley towns between Winnipeg and Minneapolis. Nelson became known in his territory for his portrayals of Hamlet, Richelieu, and Petronius in *Quo Vadis*. Another Canadian company, that of the Marks Brothers, toured at the turn of the century giving their North American audiences largely what they wanted—the melodramas that were already outdated in England and Europe. Bob Marks resolutely shunned the works of Ibsen, leaving that sort of modern play to the foreign touring companies.

Attempts to encourage Canadian dramatists in those days were very rare indeed. But one Canadian company, at least, the McDowell Company, which toured with plays by Bouçicault, Robertson and Gilbert, a repertoire heavy with melodrama, did put on two Canadian plays. Eugene McDowell was an American who formed probably the first Canadian touring company. He staged W.H. Fuller's musical, *H.M.S. Parliament,* in Emerson in 1877 and again in Montreal in 1880. Another example of McDowell's attempts to foster Canadian drama was his 1886 production of Charles Handscomb's *The Big Boom.*

The building of theatres and the visits of English and American players made possible the growth of a Canadian audience which had seen not only melodrama and variety shows but also classics from the repertoire of serious drama. It also fostered study of the art of acting. Among the Canadian actors who appeared in the nineteenth century were such accomplished players as Ida Van Cortland and Albert Tavernier. Successful Canadian dramatists, however, failed to emerge in this early period.

The history of drama in Canada shows that we are, even today, a "developing nation". It is still a question of early phases. One can point to four such phases. The first covered the early years of sporadic activity that saw few Canadian dramatists, but much theatre building and many visits by touring companies. It can be called the Indefinite Age, since it was by no means clear what, if anything, could come out of it. It began in 1606 with Lescarbot's masque of Neptune and ended with World War I. The dramatists writing in English during this period were few, and except for historical purposes are probably best forgotten. But the works of Charles Heavysege, Wilfred Campbell and Charles Mair should be mentioned as being among the first substantial efforts at Canadian drama in English. Unfortunately, the prevailing style of writing was ponderous, blank verse, full of pomposity and curious bathos which seldom went on for less than five acts. This decayed, derivative style, left over from English writing, is usually either boring or unintentionally funny. It lacks the intensity and supreme vigour of the Elizabethan style of which it is a worn-out descendant.

Heavysege, born in Huddersfield, England, in 1816, came to Canada in 1853. He worked first as a cabinet-maker and later as a journalist. His reading was mainly the Bible and Shakespeare. His play *Saul* (1857) was highly praised by such prominent men as Coventry Patmore, Emerson, Sir John A. Macdonald, and Longfellow (who held Heavysege to be the finest dramatist since Shakespeare). *Saul* was painstakingly condensed for the New York stage, but did not get a performance—the main actress died, and plans for the show collapsed.

Charles Mair, born in Lanark, Ontario, in 1838, led an adventurous life which took him all over Canada and into the thick of Louis Riel's rebellion. Mair, a fervent patriot, stressed the role of literature as a force which could help to create the consciousness of a nation. In this his thinking resembles that of the writers of the Irish Renaissance who came along at the end of the nineteenth century. Mair was convinced that the vastness of Canada held sufficient incident, scenery and character for the aspiring Canadian author. His *Tecumseh* (1886) is one of the livelier examples of nineteenth century closet drama—and this applies to English as well as Canadian closets. It is from this play that I have chosen a scene to illustrate the drama which the popular theatre of the day, with very good reason, ignored.

The reader who is curious to see a Victorian melodrama written in a style fervidly but ineptly imitative of Shakespeare, should dip into Campbell's *Mordred*. Campbell's stodgy, middle-class sensibility wreaks a sorry change on Mallory's courtly account of The King Arthur legend. It is no surprise that Campbell, as late as 1907, was silly and commonplace enough to complain of Ibsen as lacking moral sense and of Shaw as being a very un-British cynic.

One further characteristic of this phase is probably the most unfortunate of all. The influx of a vast majority of English-speaking settlers to Canada, and the struggle between French and English, led to the cultural isolation of the French Canadians. The concentration, in one region, of traditions of French culture deprived English-speaking Canada of a potentially rich and stimulating vein of experience. However, it should also be remembered that the Roman Catholic Church in French-speaking Canada did not always approve of the theatre. Monseigneur Bourget, for example, warned his flock in 1872 about the moral dangers of the Theatre Royal's activities in Montreal. Two years later he condemned all theatre activity as vicious and unworthy of attendance by respectable families. Such condemnation of touring companies and celebrities could only make things more difficult for local writers and performers who wanted secular as well as religious theatre to develop.

The second phase of the history of theatre and drama in Canada spanned the years between the two world wars. Its beginning was marked by the founding in 1919 of Hart House Theatre at the University of Toronto. This theatre was important in several ways. It was the closest thing Canada had to the small but vigorous art theatres in Europe, which were so important in bringing about a revolution in theatre and drama at the turn of the century. Hart House could not, by itself, do the same for Canada, but it continued the struggle to form audiences for serious drama by its productions and its tours of high schools. It put on Canadian plays, and it trained a couple of generations of Canadian actors and directors who have contributed immensely to the development of theatre and drama in Canada. Indeed, by the mid-twenties, Vincent Massey had enough material at his disposal to edit his two volume anthology, *Canadian Plays from Hart House Theatre* (1926-7).

A further boost for drama came suddenly and unexpectedly. In 1932 the C.B.C. was formed. Its main production centres were placed in Toronto and Montreal to broadcast English and French programmes respectively over the radio networks. This confirmed and strengthened the cultural pre-eminence of these two cities. It also provided a new medium for drama, and new jobs and experience for actors and directors. The C.B.C. rapidly built a reputation for its broadcasting of radio drama.

Further encouragement for Canadian theatre came with the establishment in 1933 of the Dominion Drama Festival. Within a system of regional and zone festivals leading to final adjudication in the national festival, little theatre groups, including university groups, competed together, thus enjoying the opportunities for comparing standards and raising them. The Dominion Drama Festival helped to arouse interest in drama across Canada, encouraged Canadian playwrights and gave amateur theatre people wider experience. It also meant that those involved worked with less sense of isolation. People across the country were able to share in a national effort.

The thirties were also significant for the drama and theatre in French Canada. Touring companies from France provided glimpses of professional work in French, but local theatre remained at the amateur level. In 1938 Father Legault founded an amateur religious theatre group, Les Compagnons de Saint-Laurent, in Quebec. This group is usually ackowledged as the source of significant modern theatre in Quebec, since it produced the people who later formed the important Théâtre du Nouveau Monde, in 1952. Side by side with the efforts of the amateurs, Roman Catholic educators were continuing to hand down the traditions of the classical French dramatists. Unfortunately, their influence has been considered one of the factors hindering the development of contemporary playwriting in Quebec. How much this was, in fact, the case is difficult to say. Canada, as a whole, was not exactly rich in playwrights during this period.

It was in French Canada that the brightest hope for the future appeared, in the person of an ebullient man of the theatre, Gratien Gélinas. He invented the character Fridolin and named his annual revue *Fridolinades*. The character became a firm favourite with the public and was a dominant figure in the world of the popular vaudeville stage and radio comedy. In the English language theatre, Merrill Denison was the main dramatist of the period, but for him the struggle was a lonely one and the future of the stage in Canada seemed bleak. This period was largely one of mediocre work in the well-worn conventions of realism and the slight one act play. We see neither new experiments nor the savage social criticism of the European avant-garde. It was, instead, the Innocuous Age.

The third phase saw the peak of radio drama and its sharp decline with the coming of C.B.C. television in 1952. In the live theatre it was the Age of Gélinas and Robertson Davies. A convenient beginning date is 1947, the year in which a neatly constructed, compassionate little comedy, *Overlaid*, announced the talent of Robertson Davies. In the following year *Tit-Coq*,

Gélinas' immensely popular play (translated in 1950, and later made into a film), offered something both distinctly Quebecois and universal in appeal. Gélinas and Marcel Dubé were the main dramatists of the period writing in French. Davies was joined by radio dramatists such as Lister Sinclair and Len Peterson, working in English. Many radio plays of this era are still unpublished.

The period is also remarkable for the growth of new theatre companies and the building of new theatres. The establishment of the Théâtre du Nouveau Monde in Montreal has already been mentioned, but Gélinas too started a company, the Comédie-Canadienne. Moreover, French Canada's oldest continuing theatre company, Théâtre du Rideau Vert, founded in 1948, had staged by the end of the sixties about a hundred different plays drawn mainly from the French, Russian, Spanish and Italian drama, and had made visits to perform in Paris.

A glance at the volumes of a bilingual publication of the Canadian Theatre Centre, *The Stage in Canada,* for the late sixties will show that by then many theatres and companies were operating, not only in Toronto and Montreal, but across the country in the main cities. In fact, they are too numerous to be mentioned here. It was also during this period of theatrical expansion that the famous Stratford Festival (1953) began. Like other important developments of this period, such as The Manitoba Theatre Centre, the Charlottetown Festival and the National Theatre School in Montreal, the Stratford Festival has played a leading part in the development of audiences for live theatre and in the demand for high, professional standards of performance and production.

By the end of the 1965-66 season the idea and the principle of state support, albeit limited, for the professional Canadian theatre had been established and was a fact. The Stratford Festival Theatre had a fame and a following outside Canada. Its use of the thrust stage has been an inspiration to other directors who feel the limitations of the proscenium arch, especially when working with plays not designed for the enclosed stage. This influence has been felt as far away as Chichester and Sheffield in England, and Minneapolis in the United States, where important new theatres have been designed with Stratford, Ontario, specifically in mind.

One characteristic of theatre in Canada during this period, (and unfortunately at the present time, as well) was the lack of real repertory companies with the chance to develop an ensemble. Actors were too often employed for only a single production. This made continuity and development difficult, and produced uncertainty about standards. But with the growth of professional theatres outside Toronto and Montreal, there has been a welcome counteraction to the draining of regional talent into those centres, and a more fertile soil now exists for Canadian dramatists.

The inauguration of the National Film Board and the Canada Film Development Corporation must also be considered for the effect of film on theatre and drama in Canada. At first sight it might seem that the theatre must suffer from falling attendance and the drain of talent into the technical and performing areas of the film world. However, actors and writers and directors who can work with film are not necessarily lost entirely to the theatre. Film work can, in fact, help to subsidize theatre ventures. Moreover, performers and audiences are brought fact to face with the fact that live performance is distinct and different from film and television. Dramatists and audiences realize that radio, television, cinema and theatre each offer different allures, all of them immensely satisfying when at their best.

In the early 1960's the experiments of such writers as James Reaney and George Ryga showed that a new kind of work could appear from Canadians writing for the stage. Ryga's plays reveal a genuine awareness of an issue special to Canada as well as to the United States—the plight of Indians whose lands and culture have been both plundered and eroded over the years. His presentation of Indian characters and their problems has involved the development of a species of dialect and a use of ballad which make the plays similar in some ways to those of the Spanish poet, Frederico Garcia Lorca

A final effect on Canadian drama of this period came from abroad. The wide popularity achieved by many of the powerful plays written in England, Europe and the United States since World War II seems to have had a beneficial impact on Canadian writing. Audiences are becoming increasingly willing to confront adult, outspoken plays with painful themes.

The fourth phase of this history is the period from the late sixties to the present, in which younger writers have been knocking at the door to take over the precarious business of writing plays. The innocuous has been left behind. We are in a phase of energetic activity among theatre groups. Many of the new theatres of the last twenty years have achieved stability, and more are springing up. University theatre departments have grown and have helped to support professional actors and to train student actors and technicians. Since the first tentative efforts of the Hart House group, theatre has come increasingly into the schools and colleges. There is enough of an established theatre in Canada now for so-called "underground theatre" to occur in Toronto, Montreal and elsewhere. Government subsidy has been forthcoming not only from the Canada Council grants, but also from the unexpected source of the Department of Manpower and the Local Initiative grants. In these small, sometimes ephemeral companies of the underground, youthful theatre people and writers can gain valuable experience.

For the dramatists, perhaps one recently formed organization holds the most significance. The Playwrights' Co-op was founded in January, 1972, with a grant from Canada Manpower in order to publish in English work by Canadian playwrights active now. The Co-op markets these plays, and also acts as an agency and advisory reading service for new playwrights.

During this period book publishers have begun to publish Canadian plays, a move they had usually been very reluctant to make in the past. The University of Toronto Press, for example, has launched the "Canadian Play Series". Among its earliest titles was David Freeman's *Creeps,* a prize-winning play of haunting power about men suffering from cerebral palsy. New Press has published work by Ryga, Reaney, Robertson Davies and a translation of Robert Gurik's experimental play, *The Hanged Man.* Further translations of French Canadian plays are promised, including works by Marcel Dubé and Michel Tremblay. Les Presses de l'Université du Québec released Etienne Duval's *Anthologie du théâtre canadien-franciais du XIXe siècle.* The courageous Talonbooks of Vancouver has begun a series of new plays, including titles by Reaney and Beverley Simons.

This present phase is a time of publication, experiment and burgeoning theatrical activity. Tameness and self-effacing attitudes have been abandoned. Clearly discernible is a willingness to comment on political and sexual matters. Indigenous Canadian tradition and consciousness is struggling harder and more urgently to forge itself. One can see these concerns embodied, for example, in David French's *Leaving Home*. In this play the situation of two sons leaving their parents' home parallels the way the family itself had left Newfoundland for urban Toronto. The contrast between the Toronto voices of the sons and the parents' accent points up the fact that the boys are in a new environment, a new world, leaving behind not only their quarrelsome father, but also perhaps, their more distant family roots.

What do these early phases of Canadian drama and theatre amount to ? It is true, there is still no genius of the Canadian theatre. But genius is very rare and very special. At the moment, it is heartening that there are now many well-equipped theatre buildings, a degree of state subsidy, and numbers of Canadian theatre people willing to stay in Canada. There are enough decently written plays about what it is like to be alive in Canada to form a basis from which new talent can continue to grow. Canadian life is now far enough removed from that of England and Europe that we need not feel so acutely the overwhelming burden of the past. Instead, today's burden is that all-too-frequent Canadian craving for American approval. That burden, too, must be shrugged off, if Canadian writers are to create works expressive of their own national consciousness, and their own kind of internationalism, using whatever forms will best dramatize them.

The problem of Canadian drama has many faces. It is a question of public money providing the equivalent of the aristocratic patronage of the past. It is a question of critical, knowledgeable, appreciative audiences. It is a question, too, of Canadian talent keeping its native cultural ties with Canada, even when it roams abroad. It is, finally, a question of waiting for genius to arise.

In 1928 Merrill Denison saw it as a melancholy and hopeless fact that " . . . the two or three indubitably Canadian plays that might be written would never find a welcome in a Canadian theatre even if there was one." Happily, there is now a Canadian theatre. And it is to the great credit of those theatre people, students and their teachers, who have worked so hard, that Denison's dispirited and unhappy words can now be forgotten.

La Guerre, Yes Sir!

Roch Carrier

Unpublished English translation by Suzanne Grossman, 1972
First production in English, Stratford, Ontario, 1972.

Part I, Scene 4
Characters in the excerpt: Joseph
Part III, Scene 2
Characters in the excerpt: Père Corriveau, Mère Corriveau, Arsène, Philibert, Sergeant, Soldiers, Amèlie, Arthur, Le Maigre, Joseph, Mme. Joseph, Josephine, Bérube, Henri

    Roch Carrier was born in 1937. He studied in New Brunswick, Montreal and Paris, and has taught at the Université de Montréal. He is resident dramatist at the Théâtre du Nouveau Monde in Montreal.
    Modern drama abounds in plays bent on opposing and satirizing the romanticism, glamour and heroics which have been associated with war. Roch Carrier's play, adapted from his novel of the same name, is a vigorous, farcical example of such drama. Full of the heady confusion and absurd accidents of war, it depicts on the one hand man's destructive drive, and on the other his redeeming will to cling stubbornly to life and love.
    The play is constructed from a series of brief, swiftly moving scenes in colloquial speech which are set in ironic contrast to one another. The mood shifts from grotesque farce to tenderness and back again to farce without warning. These scenes reveal the life of a French Canadian village overshadowed by the doom of war, a war which is literally brought home to us by the coffin of Corriveau, a villager who is blown up by a shell while answering the call of nature. The absurdity of his death is matched only by the pointlessness of the death which ends the play.
    At times, the quality of the writing is raw, falling short of the highest expectations, but in the main, the colloquial idiom captures the swift changes in mood and successfully depicts the mentality of the characters. Corriveau himself becomes the central symbol of the play, reminding us constantly of war and death; but against the squalor and cynicism of politics, Carrier sets warmth, humor and vigorous human sexuality. An engaging vitality and variety is maintained throughout the play's thirty-three scenes.
    Albert Millaire, director of the first production of the play at the Théâtre du Nouveau Monde, Montreal, in 1970, and of the subsequent tour which included Paris, Brussels, Lausanne and Prague, wrote in his program notes to the 1972 Stratford Festival performance in English:

The fact that the action of *La Guerre, Yes Sir!* takes place during the 1939-45 war never has convinced us that we were being historical. The young drama of Quebec is one of awareness; the public knows this and now insists on it. The era of sad introspection is past and humour has now found its place.

Our first excerpt, which is near the beginning of the play, shows a villager who is willing to maim himself rather than go to war. The monologue calls for great conviction and concentration from the actor. He must convince us of the reality of those two swings of the axe by the logic and the feeling of the speech, and by the physical stage business rather than by any theatre trickery. It is an astonishing scene, perfectly capturing the double theme of war fever and the stubborn will to live.

The second excerpt is a boisterous crowd scene in which the soldier's death is enacted. One is reminded of Brendan Behan's play, *The Hostage*. The action takes places in the parlour of the Corriveau house. In the room there is a table set with food and drink for the funeral of young Corriveau. Candles are burning near his coffin which rests on two logs, with chairs around it. In the wall behind the coffin there is a curtained window. A staircase leads up from the set. Bérube will appear on these stairs during the scene, wearing trousers but no shirt, and with a cap on his head.

The scene works by means of an amusing contrast of frantic action with moments of tension which lead up to and interrupt the fighting. Bitterness gives way to animal exhilaration in the battle and all gives way before the dumb bewilderment the villagers feel when the soldier is shot. Shock makes a sudden emotional vacuum, and then all the bitterness and futility of war rushes back to fill the gap.

Part I Scene 4

The village. Behind a barn. Joseph enters with an ax. He stops in front of a large tree stump.

Joseph *(calmly).* No. No. No, I won't go make their war. Their war, they can make it between themselves. The government letter . . . the government letter . . . Tiens, that's my answer to the government letter.

He places the letter on the stump and strikes with the ax.

They'll make their war without me. Me, I don't play that game.

He places his left hand on the stump and touches it with the ax. He straightens.

I like better to lose a little piece of meat here in the village than to go lose everything in the war . . . A hand, it doesn't grow back, but you don't need it to breathe.

Replacing his hand on the stump

A hand cut off, it's total security; they won't come to take me for their war. Not only that, the government will even give me a pension for disability . . . A little tap with an ax; like cutting a little branch. It's simpler than a prayer, because even if I pray, le bon Dieu's gonna let me go to war. Le bon Dieu, he doesn't seem to be against the war.

Shifting his ax to the left hand and placing the right on the stump

Which hand? Got to think of the future. The right, that's my best hand; the hardest worker, the strongest . . . and it likes to caress the woman . . . I'll keep the right.

Changing hands

>It looks so pitiful, a hand all alone . . . Ah! their maudite war makes men into jam. Jam . . . I'll make jam in the autumn, while they make their war; strawberry jam, blueberry jam, currant jam, crab-apple jam, raspberry jam, blackberry jam . . . Han!

The ax strikes, the hand is severed. Blood. He exits, sobbing.

>It doesn't hurt! It doesn't hurt! . . . It doesn't hurt.

Part III, Scene 2

Corriveau house set. Joseph throws open the door. He enters, followed by the villagers in an angry mood.

Sergeant. Attention!

Joseph. Les maudits Anglais, they've taken everything from us, but they won't get our Corriveau. They won't get the last night of Corriveau.

Josephine. We want our Corriveau!

Mme. Joseph. You won't take our Corriveau!

Père Corriveau *(to Joseph).* You, Joseph, cut off your hands if you want, cut off your head if you want, but don't make any trouble here.

Mère Corriveau *(pot in hand).* It's from the stove. It's red. If I hit you, your teeth'll burn.

Sergeant. Here it comes!

They obey.

Arsène. I don't feel like fighting no more.

Arthur. You won't have our Corriveau.

Joseph. Go back to your maudite England, maudits Anglais.

Mme. Joseph. There's a train at noon. Take it and don't get off till you're in England.

Amelie. He's handsome, that one. It's too bad he's Anglais.

Arthur. He's a Christ d'Anglais.

Le Maigre. They're not even real Anglais. They come to Canada because the real Anglais don't want them.

Josephine. You don't get our Corriveau.

Joseph. Our Corriveau, it's *our* Corriveau.

Père Corriveau and Mère Corriveau stand aside.

Père Corriveau. You can't say he's wrong.

Mère Corriveau *(sadly).* My boy's gonna have to be under the ground before he has peace.

The villagers approach the soldiers. They pull their ears, their hair, poke them with curiosity. The soldiers are at attention, reluctant to fight.

Joseph. Baptême, they don't move, ces Anglais-là. They're dead.

Amélie. I wonder if their little thing looks like a little thing Canadien-français.

Arthur. Amélie, don't cheat on me en anglais.

Sergeant. God-damned animals. Let's go boys!

Battle Royal. The Corriveaus retreat with their bottles and casseroles.

Mère Corriveau. It's war!

Père Corriveau. Yes Sir.

Mme. Joseph. We're gonna take back our Corriveau. *(to soldier)* Don't touch me, I'll bite you!

Sergeant. Let's get the bastards!

Josephine. Napoléon! Help!

Arsène. Maudit. Why do we always have to fight?

Le Maigre. If we want our Corriveau, we'll get him.

Joseph. Christ! If I'd known, I would have waited till tomorrow to cut my hand.

Josephine. When you're not there, Napoléon, I feel all alone.

Joseph. Where do you want it? In the teeth or in the nose?

Arthur. You want to die here or do I kick you to England?

Amélie. Oie, oie, he's tickling me!

Josephine. They have hands soft as Napoléon.

Le Maigre. Maudit country. It's always the same ones that get beaten up.

Mme. Joseph. Joseph, he wants to do things!

Joseph. Zeldina, don't let them paw you!

Mme. Joseph. Don't be jealous of those who have two hands . . .

Josephine. Oh! My gums are bleeding.

Arthur. They'll bleed.

Arsène. Like my pigs?

Amélie. He wants to rape me.

Bérube appears on the stairs, dressed as before.

Bérube. Ah! Saint-Chrême! *(He leaps into the fray.)*

Sergeant *(seeing him).* Attention!

Soldiers, including Berube, come to attention.

Sergeant. Private, you're going to help us teach these people a lesson. That's an order.

Bérube fights on the army's side. The fight continues.

Henri rushes through the door into the room.

Henri. Corriveau, I see you, I'll shoot you!

A shot. Everybody freezes. The villagers part and Henri stands dumbly facing a dead soldier. The sergeant is at the soldier's side. He rises slowly.

Sergeant. Who did it? Who killed my soldier? *(He moves to Henri who is frozen in shock, removes his rifle.)*

Sergeant. By Christ, you'll pay for this.

The villagers close in to defend Henri. Bérube stands apart.

Sergeant *(to Henri).* I'll shoot you all myself, you sons of bitches.

Joseph. They shouldn't have attacked us!

Sergeant. I'll see you hanged. Every last bloody one of you.

The villagers form a wall in front of Henri.

Sergeant. Pick the boy up.

The body is moved beside the coffin, with the rifle that killed him.

Le Maigre. Maudite war. You just have to think the word and men fall to the ground like flies.

The Killdeer

James Reaney

First published 1962
First production, Toronto, 1960, by Coach House Theatre

From Act III, Scene 1
Characters in the excerpt: Madam Fay, Mrs. Budge, Harry, Eli

James Reaney was born in 1926 not far from Stratford, Ontario. He studied English at University College, Toronto, and won an Epstein award for his poetry and short stories. He took his M.A. in English in 1949 and in the same year published *The Red Heart,* which received the Governor General's Award for the best volume of poetry that year. He later gained his Ph.D. and taught English in various universities. He founded and edited the magazine *Alphabet,* has written a number of prize-winning books, and has had several works performed on C.B.C. Radio and Television.

The Killdeer, a play in verse, was first performed in January 1960 at the Coach House Theatre in Toronto. The killdeer of Reaney's title is a bird which cries before a storm and decoys predators from its nestlings. As in Ibsen's *The Wild Duck* and Chekhov's *The Seagull,* the bird is the central symbol, and associated particularly with a female character. In Reaney's play, the killdeer is associated with the girl, Rebecca. She is tried for killing Clifford, an orphan, and is later released.

Our scene shows the fabulous and fearsome Madam Fay, cosmetics saleslady extraordinary, revealing some of the weird, savage relationships which haunt this surreal comedy of the dark reaches of human personality. The challenges of the scene are various: the speaking of the verse itself; the presentation of the volatile, witchlike Madam Fay; the sudden switching from emotional intensity to hysterical climax, mockery and laughter. Most of the scene is a dialogue, but could easily become a monologue by Madam Fay if one were to select a passage from among her speeches. The action of the play occurs in rural Ontario.

Mrs. Gardner's parlour. Harry and Eli are living in it. There are dead leaves on the floor and we hear the wind whistling. Harry, wearing an apron, is busy preparing supper and Eli is sitting in one of the Gardners' chairs.

Harry. Eli, you haven't been out all day.

Eli. No. I haven't, Harry.

Harry. Why don't you take a walk before supper?

Eli. It's got too dark.

Harry. It's got too dark.

Eli. Yes, and anyhow I looked out and there's a woman standing in the shadows at the end of the street.

Harry. She's nothing to be afraid of. It's only one of my mother's friends. Mrs. Budge. I've told you about her and her son. I don't know why she doesn't go inside somewhere.

Eli. This wasn't that old woman. This was another woman. My mother.

Harry. I doubt that. I really think she's vanished for good. I don't even think she'll turn up for the trial tomorrow.

Eli. I saw her tracks in the snow yesterday. She's back all right.

Harry. Eli, I want you to go out and get me a quart of milk.

Eli. I won't Harry. I can't.

Harry. And there's an extra nickel for candy.

Eli. No.

Harry. One extra nickel for candy.

Eli. All right, Harry. You trapped me. I'll go. I'll sneak out the back way.

Harry. Here's the bottle. I want you to get used to going out, Eli. If you stop—Lord knows what could happen next. *(Eli goes out.)* You might have to get yourself a box and shut down the lid like a dead jack-in-the-box. That might very well be. That might very well be. *(He retreats into the kitchen.)*

Madam Fay *(Entering and inspecting the whole house, kitchen and all. She comes in with the apron Harry has just been wearing.)* Anybody home? Nobody? Well, I'll wait. I'll wait for you, Eli. *(She lights a cigarette and turns her back to the door. Mrs. Budge enters furtively.)* Who is it?

Madam Fay. Who is it? It isn't Harry Gardner. It isn't my son Eli. So who is it?

Mrs. Budge.   Oh begging your pardon, Madam Fay,
But I happened to be passing by and I saw the light.
A very dear friend of mine once lived here—
Mrs. Vinnie Gardner. You may remember her. I thought
That this place was not lived in any longer.

Madam Fay. Oh it's lived in. Harry Gardner and my son
Have been living here the last six months.
I've got something I want to tell my son
When he comes back here with his fancy friend.

Mrs. Budge. Is it that brought you into town, Madam Fay?

Madam Fay. That jerk had me subpoenaed to be a witness tomorrow

When they re-try that wretched girl. I have to be there!
How she managed to have a baby and delay things
So she didn't get hanged last September is a holy miracle.

Mrs. Budge. You see it was. Otherwise she'd be dead by now.

Madam Fay. And so she should be. The vicious little monster.
Hey! How'd you get out? Isn't your address the poorhouse?

Mrs. Budge. Yes. But I couldn't bear it no longer. The potatoes
Went rotten and we've been picking them over
In the cellar.

Madam Fay. So that's what that's like.
I suppose I'll be there too in twenty years.
You've let your face go too far, old woman, I think—
What are you looking at?

Mrs. Budge. You. I've heard
So much about you. I never felt it possible
That I'd meet you.

Madam Fay. What'd you hear about me?

Mrs. Budge. How wicked you are.

Madam Fay. I suppose you're good!

Mrs. Budge. No. I'm wicked too. I'm black as pitch.

Madam Fay. Blacker than me?

Mrs. Budge. I killed my son. Have you killed yours?

Madame Fay. Not yet
How do you mean you killed your son?

Mrs. Budge. I pushed him.
I pushed him into a river that slid through a jungle.

Madam Fay. You're so old you're not afraid to show your secret heart.

Mrs. Budge. I've come so far down the river of time it don't matter.

Madam Fay. Would you like to see my secret heart?
There's something I've never told anybody
And I want to tell it—it relieves the horror.

Mrs. Budge. What's in your heart, your secret heart. Is it a frog?
Or a king and a queen killed in a cellar?
Or a starved rat? Or a mess of gray beetles?
Or a large fat snail? Or is it wild men dancing round a fire?

Madam Fay *(after pausing to see that no one is listening).*
Look! Do you see there into my heart? What do you see?

Mrs. Budge. It's a little snapshot of two young girls about ten.

Madam Fay. Yes, yes. I was an orphan girl. An orphan from here.
They wanted another little girl to keep theirs company.
I hated her the moment I saw her. I loved her too.
Do you know who she was?

Mrs. Budge.   Rebecca's mother.

Madam Fay. Right. She was the mother—my foster-sister was—
Of this Rebecca who's being tried again tomorrow
For the murder of the one man I ever loved.

Mrs. Budge. So that's who you loved—really. This Clifford Hopkins.

Madam Fay. He was an orphan boy at the other farm. The Fay farm.
When he was twelve he met me on the road.
As I was coming home from school. Where was she?
He asked me to go down into the ditch with him.
That's the man this Rebecca claims she killed.
Thank God the poor fool finally owned that store.
He spent his whole life wanting to own something.

Mrs. Budge. Should he have?

Madam Fay.   By the time he did it was too late.
God! If you could have seen his secret heart—
Like the tusk of a wild pig growing into its eye—
The more power he got the worse he felt.
But we—Rebecca's mother and I—were once two girls
Together. We slept in the same room. We walked, linked
Arm in arm. She loved me. I hated her for that.
Because it was so easy for her and I couldn't—love me.
Once in the fields she found a killdeer bird
That had a broken wing.

Mrs. Budge   Is that the bird
That flies in over the town crying its name
When it's going to rain?

Madam Fay.   She did all she could
For this bird did Rebecca's ma. Everything. One morning
I got up real early, crept to the woodshed—I opened
The door of its cage and I struck it with a stick of wood.

Mrs. Budge. Why did you do that?

Madam Fay.   I don't know, Granny!
I just had to kill it. All of a sudden she was there
And it flew to her and disappeared and she went away.
Then came back. As if nothing had happened. Sweet—

Mrs. Budge. Then you were sorry for your evil ways.

Madam Fay. I felt the ground had turned to whetted knives.
I waited for her to say something. She didn't.
My own badness was like a rotting thing.
I could smell it. I knew now the one thing I
Wanted in the world was for her to break the spell.
To come at me—hit me over and over again.
For what I'd done. Then I'd stop hating her.
I would love her. I would be her sister. I would
Be their child . . . But it never came.
She didn't love me enough even to hate me—
There was this abominable smell. I fell ill.
She slept, but I didn't. I got up and went to her dress.
In the pocket there was still the dead bird.
She'd rather have a dead thing crawling with worms
Than break the shell of evil I lay hatching in.
I took the dress and I burnt it—and the next week
He asked me down into the ditch. Oh she tried—
She tried to say she was sorry, but it was no use.
She'd let me
See that nothing I did made the least difference to her.
I didn't want her forgiveness. I wanted her anger,
The proof that she could be as evil as me.
How can you grab hold of light with arms of dark!
No, the light must give us a stair of darkness first.
(to herself)
Well, I have your killdeer now and I'll torture it
Till your ghost comes from the grave and
Annihilates me with hatred.

Mrs. Budge. You know something that would save her daughter?

Madam Fay. And how sharp you are, old woman. After that she married.
I got married. I had two men. She had only one.
Eventually her man asked me to elope with him.

Mrs. Budge. Whose child is your Eli then? The one that murdered
Or the one that got murdered. Fay or Hopkins?

Madam Fay. I had nothing to do with Hopkins while I was married.
I even managed for about two years before
To virgin up somewhat. What do you think I am?
An absolute whore? So I got her husband.
I lost my husband. And then I lost her husband.
She had this daughter—Rebecca, sweet and bonny.
I had this son of mine—the touchy, frightened runt.
But my son married her daughter and ruined her life
So I get her daughter and so she had nothing.
And then she up and claims to have murdered
My Clifford.

Mrs. Budge. Well, who did kill him?

Madam Fay. You look at me as if I might have killed him.
Do you think I killed him?

Mrs. Budge. No.

Madam Fay. You'd better say 'No' or I'll twist your head off.
I haven't seen Clifford Hopkins for ten years.
No—and then her dear sweet forgiving daughter
Tells the police *she* killed him. Oh what a female Jesus.
Always suffering for others. I hope she hangs. Let her.

Mrs. Budge. But why would Rebecca say she'd murdered Hopkins
If she didn't?

Madam Fay. Because she's shielding somebody.

Mrs. Budge. Who is she shielding?

Madam Fay. Why my son Eli, of course.

Mrs. Budge. Did your son murder Clifford Hopkins then?

Madam Fay. Granny, I know he murdered Hopkins. I know he did.

Mrs. Budge. Woman, you must speak out!
You mustn't let an innocent girl go to her death!

Madam Fay. Oh, but I will let her go. I'm going to
Let her hang! I'm going to hit her one!
Oh Rebecca if I kill your daughter will you
Send me your hatred soon. Send me Hell
To consume me. To eat the wounded bird,
I don't want my wing to be fixed. I want
You to take a stick of wood and beat me to death!
Rebecca! Rebecca! *(She writhes on the floor and screams, terrifying Mrs. Budge. Then gets up and laughs.)*
Look at her! She wants to have a run. With what she
Knows. Now there's nothing I like better if it's not
Smashing up birds with broken wings and letting
Innocent young ladies get hanged than chasing
Old ladies down wet slippery dark streets. Yahoo!
I'll give you a head start to the poorhouse.
And when you get there—right at the gate—I'll
Leap out at you.

Budge disappears, Fay about to pursue, but Fay sees Eli coming, so enters parlour again, looks for hiding-place, then runs into kitchen.

Nobody Waved Goodbye

Don Owen

Published 1966
First released 1964

Characters in the excerpt: Peter, Ron

Film maker Don Owen held a Canada Council arts award for 1966-67. His *Notes for a Film on Donna and Gail* (National Film Board, 1966) won a *grand prix* for middle-length films at the Montreal International Film Festival, 1966. He also made *The Ernie Game* (N.F.B., 1967).

Nobody Waved Goodbye, one of his earlier films, was an international award winner. A modest, low-budget picture, it was acclaimed for the acting of Peter Kastner and Julie Biggs. It was also notable for its use of the technique known as *cinéma verité,* which creates an impression that the camera is a voyeur, and the sound apparatus is eavesdropping on spontaneous life.

The film explores the problems of Peter, a teenager determined to make himself independent of the qualifications derby, and the middle-class rat-race. Owen uses none of the expensive and not necessarily effective elaborations of Hollywood. His structure is eminently cinematic. Short scenes cross-cut, one to another, long shots zoom into close-up, the camera dollies, and pictures dissolve. Dialogue is terse, colloquial, and improvisational.

When the film was released in Canada in 1964 it made no great impression on Canadian audiences. But early in 1965 it made a hit with American reviewers, who saw that the acting was very good, and that Peter was a more complex figure than the usual mixed-up youth on the well-worn slope to delinquency. He is likeable, intelligent, at times honest, and not entirely blameworthy. His fate is partly a result, of course, of the society in which he lives.

The scene presented here, though seemingly casual and undramatic, poses the central issue of the film. We are given a glimpse of Peter's capacity for honest questioning of social issues, a quality which could have made him a responsible member of society. But his manner has something of that aggressiveness and arrogance which led to his final evasion of responsibility and made him too weak to be a courageous social critic. Set in the living room of Peter's home, the scene has that air of spontaneity so typical of the film, in which it seemed as if the crew just happened to be in the house at the time and managed to work unseen. As the author has avoided the easy crutches of melodrama and hypertension, the particular challenge for the actors is to make something fairly low key and not very remarkable convincing and gripping.

Medium Shot: Peter and Ron.

Peter *(indignantly).* Oh! Parents! Sit down! Listen!

Peter sits on chair. Ron sits down on couch across from him.

Peter. I mean . . . I'd like to ask you . . . Are you happy with the set-up . . . like the way things are going for you now? *(Pause.)* Have you got what you want? *(Pause.)* Are you satisfied?

Ron. No . . . *(He pauses for a moment, thinking.)* I'm still working for it.

Peter. What exactly are you working for? You've been through college. You've got a great practice. You make a lot of money. You're putting teeth in people. Is that what you . . . is that what the whole thing was for?

Ron *(smiling).* I'm doing what I want to do and I'm making a good living out of it. What's wrong with that?

Peter *(persistently).* I mean . . . did you ever stop to take a look at the kind of life you were leading? Did you ever stop to sort of consider it and consider your values and the things you were living for? Did you ever really? No, I mean, did you? Or did you sort of live without any goal or any reason for it?

Ron does not respond. He sits looking at Peter indulgently, smoking his pipe.

Peter. I bet, that's the kind of thing . . . that's the kind of life you live isn't it? You just, I mean . . . why are you going to *Cleopatra* tonight? Why do you waste seven bucks? Just because everyone else is doing it!

Ron *(irritated).* Peter, you know, you are getting a little obnoxious!

Peter. No . . . no, I mean . . . don't! Isn't it the truth? Don't you ever get that, that's what you are doing?

Ron *(angrily).* No, I didn't come here to sit down and get insulted by you.

Peter *(insistently).* Listen! Why are you going to *Cleopatra* anyway? Just because of all the publicity, and the pictures all over of Elizabeth Taylor. Isn't that the reason?

Ron *(patronizingly).* Peter, if you had a hard time with your parents about skipping school, don't take it out on me brother, because I don't want this . . .

Peter *(interrupting him).* I'm not taking it out on you, but, you know, I can't understand guys like you. I mean . . . I just can't understand your way of life. All you're worried about is the buck. That's all! That's all you stand on your feet all day long for . . . is to get some money, to get some more money . . . to get some more money. Isn't that what you do all day?

Ron. Peter, why don't you go and study?

Medium shot: Peter.

Peter *(angrily).* I will. I'll go and study right now.

The Labyrinth

Charles Israel

Published 1969
Televised 1963, on C.B.C.

Scene 6
Characters in the excerpt: Hester, Abbie

Charles Israel was born in the United States in 1920, but has lived in Canada since 1953. He is a prolific writer for radio, television and film. His C.B.C. Television play about Christ's resurrection, *The Open Grave,* won the city of Genoa Award in 1964. In a French version, it won the Best Scenario Award, when shown at the Prague Film Festival of 1965.

In *The Labyrinth,* first seen on C.B.C. Television in 1963, his concern with young people is combined with an equal concern for the problems of the disturbed individual. While various locations are used in the play—a snack bar, a bachelor apartment, a club in the country—the most important setting is the maze, from which the title of the play is derived. The maze set is at once suggestive of the intricacies of the mind, different areas of time, an institution for disturbed youngsters and the winding path of psychiatric therapy. This symbolic setting and Abbie's frequent dashing through it, fairly novel things for television in 1963, enable the action to shift about in time without the usual flashback. Compare this with the use of setting and time in Ryga's *Ecstasy of Rita Joe.*

The main action of the play is the progress of Abbie's therapy, her groping for a way out of the maze. In our excerpt she is outside the maze in a snack bar where she reveals something of the chronic insecurity she tries to hide. She inexpertly plays the role of a sophisticated woman of the world in front of Hester, her timid friend.

The setting is the interior of a snack bar. In contrast to the sets we have seen so far, this one is fairly detailed and realistic. Abbie makes her way to the booth where Hester is sitting. She is Abbie's age, but plain and ungainly. Her clothes do nothing for her or anyone else. She worships Abbie, who accepts the idolatry as her due. And as is usually the case with such relationships, it brings out the worst in Abbie. As soon as Hester sees Abbie approaching, she smiles radiantly and a little pathetically, half-rising and waiting like a small dog determining the mood of a beloved master.

Hester has finished one malted and is working on another. Across the table from her are a hamburger and a malted, untouched.

Hester. Hi, Abbie. I thought you weren't ever coming.

Abbie. Oh, have you been waiting long? I'm sorry. *(She isn't.)*

Hester. I ordered something for you. It looked good when it came to the table. But I guess it's cold now.

Abbie. I'm not hungry anyhow. You have it.

With eager obedience, Hester pulls the hamburger and malted across the table and attacks them. Abbie takes out a pack of cigarettes, lights one, takes a clumsy puff, and blows out smoke world-wearily.

Abbie. It's been such a trying day.

Hester *(with mouth full).* I'm dying to hear what you have to tell me.

Abbie. Hester, for heaven's sake, how often do I have to tell you not to talk with your mouth full? It's so ungracious.

Hester. I'm sorry. *(Her eyes bug as she swallows mightily.)* What was it you had to tell me?

Abbie. Did I have something to tell you?

Hester *(disappointed).* You said you did. Don't you? *(Brightens.)* Is it about the literary club?

Abbie *(as if she smells something bad).* The literary club?

Hester. Oh. Then it must be about a boy. Tommy—

Abbie. Tommy? That child?

Hester. He's seventeen.

Abbie. Really, Hester. *(Can't keep it any longer.)* If you must know, I have a date with Kenneth tonight.

Hester. Kenneth Shraft?

Abbie. Of course. He's been bugging me and bugging me to go out with him, and finally just to shut him up I said I would.

Hester. But he must be twenty-three. Or even twenty-four. And he's divorced.

Abbie *(puffing clumsily on her cigarette).* I like experienced men.

Hester. Your mother won't let you go.

Abbie. I met him at a church social, didn't I? It's not like—

Hester. But he's been married.

Abbie. You do have to be married before you can get a divorce, you know. Hester, sometimes you are tedious. Give me a sip.

Hester pushes the malted over to Abbie, who takes a scornful but healthy sip, then pushes the glass back.

Hester. I remember last summer when I used to watch you and Kenneth playing tennis. The way he looked at you all the time, it was kind of creepy. I'd be scared to go out with him.

Abbie *(cruelly).* But you're not going out with him, are you?

Hester. I wouldn't go even if he asked me.

Abbie. Wouldn't you?

Hester. Oh, I know he's good-looking and a cool dancer and all that. But I wouldn't know how to act, and besides my mother would never let me go out with anybody that much older, and I'd be scared, Abbie . . . Abbie . . .

While Hester is speaking, Abbie is looking toward camera, her head averted from her friend's gaze. Abbie's eyes are growing troubled, a little frightened.

Abbie *(thoughtfully).* Hester . . .

Hester. Uh-huh?

Abbie. Hester, I . . . *(She means to tell Hester she's scared, too, but can't bring herself to admit it.)* Nothing. You wouldn't understand.

Hester. Oh, I would, Abbie, I would.

Abbie *(sudden bitterness).* Would you? Would anybody?

Hester stares at her, puzzled and disturbed. Abbie gets up. Hester gulps down the last of the malted and follows her, finds that Abbie has stopped near the juke box, where she stands lost in thought.

Hester. Where do you think Kenneth will take you?

Abbie *(absently).* Oh, I don't know. Some smart supper club, probably, or one of those fancy bars where you can dance. But I've just been thinking, maybe I won't go out with him after all.

Hester. You won't?

Abbie. If he wants a date bad enough, he can wait a while.

Hester. You're right, Abbie, keep him hanging.

Abbie. And he *is* a lot older.

Hester. Sure.

Abbie. And these characters that've been married . . .

Hester. That's right.

Abbie. Maybe when I get home I'll call him and—

Hester. Abbie . . .

Abbie. Hmm?

Hester. Well . . . if you're not going out with Kenneth . . . I mean, for a while anyhow . . . I mean, I met him once, but . . . do you think you could introduce me . . .

Abbie. I thought you said—

Hester *(miserably).* Yes, but if you—

Abbie turns fiercely on her heel and walks toward the door.

Hester. Abbie, where are you going?

Abbie *(calls back).* To get ready for *my* date. Tell you all about it . . . sometime.

Charbonneau and Le Chef

John Thomas McDonough

First published 1968
First broadcast 1968, on C.B.C. Radio

Act II, Scene 1
Characters in the excerpt: Charbonneau, Courtevue, Le Chef

    J.T. McDonough was a Dominican Father and now teaches philosophy at Centennial College, Scarborough. *Charbonneau and Le Chef* was produced for radio by Robert Weaver, and a recording on disc is available from C.B.C. The play has also been performed in French at La Salle Crémazie in the Grande Théâtre in Quebec City (1970).
    The historical background to the play is the bitter and violent strike of 1949 in the small mining town of Asbestos, about forty-five miles to the east of Montreal. Monseigneur Joseph Charbonneau, Archbishop of Montreal, took the side of the workers, helping them to conclude a settlement for higher pay, and safer, healthier working conditions. This represented a defeat both for the mining firms and for the provincial government led by Premier Duplessis, or "Le Chef" as he was often called. Charbonneau was later dismissed, as a result, it has been said, of pressure exerted on the Church authorities by Duplessis. Such controversial events and behind-the-scenes struggles add up to power-plays, personality clashes and ideological conflicts which are the stuff of drama.
    The demands of historical accuracy are not necessarily those of the theatre. Events so recent cannot be used in the theatre as easily as those from the distant past without incurring charges of bias and propaganda for the writer. McDonough's play, therefore, has linking passages of narrated explanation which alert us to background and events not used in the dramatic scenes.
    The scenes printed here have considerable force and impact. The characterization and development of the two symmetrical arguments conveying the conflict of an individual Christian conscience with the hierarchical establishments of the Church and the Government are what make the excerpt such good acting material. The two attempts to silence Charbonneau, one by his fiery colleague, the other by the wily and worldly politician, make a splendid contrast. There is also a symmetry of rhetoric and passion. Notice, too, that here is a political drama of ideas which is also one of personal motives: those which underlie Courtevue's inability to appreciate Charbonneau's viewpoint, and those which drive Le Chef to obtain the Bishop's tacit support or else "conspire his overthrow".

Monseigneur Charbonneau is dressed in a black cassock, ceintured with a red sash. On his head is perched a skull cap; around his neck hangs a pectoral cross. He is fifty-seven years old, enormous in size, over six feet six inches tall. Everything about him, beginning with his strong handsome face, suggests strength—physical strength, intellectual strength, and spiritual strength. He seems capable of any kind of endurance or endeavour.

Scattered around his room, on shelves, chairs, and on the floor, are numerous books, periodicals, and newspapers, evidence of the Archbishop's interest in learning. A large oil painting of Pope Pius XII hangs on the wall, above and behind a wide-tabled mahogany desk.

Courtevue. Your sermon in Notre Dame, last Sunday, was outrageous, simply disgraceful . . .

Charbonneau *(calm)*. Careful, Monseigneur Courtevue, you might smash my desk with that huge fist of yours, careful.

Courtevue *(striking the desk harder)*. Never mind your desk. I'm concerned with the well-being of our Church. I say your sermon was disgraceful, and harmful to the—

Charbonneau *(calm)*. Calm yourself, Monseigneur, calm yourself! Disgraceful is hardly the word to describe my stand last Sunday.

Courtevue *(still shouting)*. With that outrageous sermon of yours, you placed the whole Church in an awkward position.

Charbonneau. Awkward position?

Courtevue. You attacked openly the policies of our government.

Charbonneau. So . . . ?

Courtevue *(hits the desk a hard blow)*. Why this is out-and-out defiance of rightful and legitimate authority. You—

Charbonneau *(firmly)*. I did what I thought was right. *(He stares at him, holding his eyes for a moment.)* I'd expect any Archbishop to do the same. It's our duty to defend the weak and the oppressed against social injustice.

Courtevue *(impatient)*. That's not the point, all of the bishops are helping the strikers, and all of our priests. You are not alone in the fight for social justice. That's not the point, you hear!

Charbonneau *(calm)*. What is the point?

Courtevue *(shaking an accusing finger)*. The point is you always act alone, independently of your colleagues . . . Why, if you carry on in this way, you will lead the French Church, in Quebec, into a schism.

Charbonneau. Nonsense, I know what is expected of me as an archbishop.

Courtevue. You are a proud man, Monseigneur Charbonneau. You always think you are right and everybody else wrong. It's sinful pride. That's what it is . . sinful pride.

Charbonneau *(annoyed)*. Don't be so self-righteous, Monseigneur Courtevue. You have no right to sit in judgement on me.

Courtevue *(scolding, threatening)*. Now listen to me, you rash young man.

Charbonneau *(smiling)*. Thank you for the compliment, Monseigneur. At fifty-seven years old, it is nice to be called a young man.

Courtevue *(irritated)*. Don't be facetious with me . . . You must learn more respect for the opinions of your colleagues, especially your elders.

Charbonneau. Frankly, I am concerned with the implementation of social justice in this province, not with pleasing my colleagues. I—

Courtevue *(impatient)*. Why do you always pose as a lone crusader. You're not the only bishop concerned with justice . . . We are all concerned with the problems of justice. But the other bishops don't like your radical interpretations of justice.

Charbonneau *(calm)*. I respect the right of my colleagues to express their sincere opinions. But I can't very well give my support to policies and programs, which, in my opinion, smack of obscurantism and narrow-minded bigotry. I—

Courtevue *(solemn)*. Defending the Church against heresy and your revolutionary social theories is hardly bigotry, Monseigneur Charbonneau.

Charbonneau *(fed up)*. Here we go again, another childish argument, another useless polemic. It's always the same when you and I meet. We never seem to find a common ground for agreement. We invariably end up insulting each other.

Courtevue. As long as you refuse to attend the annual meetings of the bishops, I shall continue to distrust your motives and your policies. I warn you, I can take measures to force you to be less independent. I can—

Charbonneau *(raising his voice)*. I don't care what measures you take. *(He slams his fist on his desk.)* I have more important things to do than to waste my precious time in endless discussions which lead nowhere. Every time I open my mouth, at the bishops' meetings, you and your friends attack me and insult me. Monseigneur Roy of Quebec is the only Archbishop who sides with me. He—

Courtevue. He's a fence-sitter.

Charbonneau. He understands what I'm trying to do for the Church in this province.

Courtevue. In that case, I shall keep an eye on him too . . .

Charbonneau *(angry, rising from his desk)*. You are too short-sighted to play the role of commissar effectively, Monseigneur. And I don't care whom you keep your eyes on I intend to speak my mind. Until the Asbestos Strike is settled, I am going to use all my influence to protect the workers from the tyranny of our present government. This you can report to whomever you wish. Do you understand me?

Courtevue. This is a dangerous and imprudent course of action, I warn you.

Charbonneau *(turning away from him)*. Rubbish . . .

Courtevue *(deadly serious)*. We must avoid, at all costs, an out-and-out confrontation with the government.

Charbonneau *(sharply)*. At all costs, Your Excellency? *(He sits down again at his desk.)*

Courtevue *(toning down his voice, showing discomfiture)*. Well . . . it's all right to help the workers and the strikers, in the proper spirit of Christian Charity. I'm all for this . . . but surely there was no need for you to attack the government and industry, as you did. This is, to say the least, rash and imprudent behaviour for an Archbishop. Why this is—

Charbonneau *(impatient)*. Rubbish, rubbish, you don't understand what is happening in Quebec. Quebec is undergoing an industrial revolution. Quebec is no longer an agricultural society. We must tell the people to vote for a new labour code, otherwise we shall live to see a violent rebellion in this province.

Courtevue. The Asbestos Strike is a rebellion.

Charbonneau. Not quite, just the beginnings of a quiet revolution . . .

Courtevue *(showing alarm)*. Beginnings of a quiet revolution?

Charbonneau. This strike will force the government to revise its social legislation.

Courtevue *(hitting the desk with his fist)*. There is nothing basically wrong with the present social legislation.

Charbonneau. Monseigneur Courtevue, you are living in the past. Our social legislation is a hundred years behind the times. Believe me, I know. I have studied economics and sociology in the States. I—

Courtevue *(acidly)*. That's the trouble with you, you have lived too long abroad. You don't understand the people of Quebec. Your roots in this province, are not deep and strong like mine. Your ideas and feelings are alien.

Charbonneau. Alien?

Courtevue. Yes . . . Anglo-Saxon and Protestant.

Charbonneau *(snapping back)*. My roots are as strong and deep as your own. And besides, it doesn't matter whether my ideas are alien or popular. What does matter is whether they are true.

Courtevue. You are presumptuous in believing that your ideas are always true.

Charbonneau *(firmly)*. You can't argue with facts, Monseigneur. And I know for a fact that compared to the social legislation of the States and English Canada our Quebec legislation is primitive and barbaric. And that's what's disgraceful; not my sermon last Sunday.

Courtevue *(angry).* You are disloyal to your own people. The social legislation of this province was drawn up by a respectable, civilized Catholic government, which is mindful of the teachings of the Church.

Charbonneau *(quietly).* The government is mindful more of power than justice.

Courtevue *(long pause. He paces the room, glancing at books and pictures. He is obviously angry).* You miss my point.

Charbonneau. I'm always missing your point. What now are you aiming at?

Courtevue *(very solemn).* Our French Catholic Church cannot survive in this Protestant country—without the help and support of a strong Catholic government.

Charbonneau *(calmly).* I still don't get your point.

Courtevue *(impatient, speaking rapidly).* I'll spell it out for you then: if our government ever begins to tax our Church properties, all is lost . . .

Charbonneau. Why should the government tax our properties?

Courtevue. Because of prelates like you.

Charbonneau. Because of me?

Courtevue. Yes, because of you and your rash meddling in politics.

Charbonneau. I have never meddled in politics. It's against my principles. I—

Courtevue. Your sermon last Sunday was a direct attack on the government. The Prime Minister has threatened to retaliate by depriving the Church of its much-needed revenues.

Charbonneau *(bored).* So what?

Courtevue *(shocked).* Good God, man, don't you see what will happen?

Charbonneau *(affecting to read some of the correspondence on his desk).* I fail to see any real threat to God's Church . . .

Courtevue *(exhorting).* Why, we will be forced to close our schools, our colleges, our seminaries, even our Churches . . .

Charbonneau *(sharply hitting his desk).* What good are schools, colleges seminaries, even Churches, if we can't speak freely in them, and teach truth and justice to the people?

Courtevue *(shouting).* They are necessary for the teaching of religion.

Charbonneau. You mean a soulless religion.

Courtevue *(barking back).* Are you implying that the catholic religion is soulless?

Charbonneau. Any religion, without faith, courage, and commitment, is dead and meaningless. That's what I mean.

Courtevue *(shocked).* The Catholic Church meaningless . . . why you . . .

Charbonneau *(rising from his chair, walking over to Courtevue, facing him).* You attach too much importance to prestige and money. The life of Christ's Church is not grounded on state-supported institutions but on the faith of the people. Where there is faith there is a Church . . .

Courtevue. Now you sound like a Protestant.

Charbonneau. I am simply quoting Saint Paul.

Courtevue. But naturally . . . he's the Patron Saint of the Protestants.

Charbonneau. I always thought he was the Apostle to the Gentiles.

Courtevue *(shaking his head).* Sometimes I doubt whether you have the faith . . . You think and act like a heretic.

Charbonneau *(angry).* And sometimes I doubt whether you have any brains. You think and act like an illiterate farmer from Lac St. Jean.

Courtevue. Like a farmer, why you insolent, you . . . arrogant heretic . . . you . . .

Charbonneau. Listen to me! I govern a cosmopolitan diocese, not a country parish. In my territory there are a million proletarians, and I'm not going to deal with them as though they lived in a little rural village like your diocese of Rimouski. You want me to dress up my grown men in the short pants of your little boys . . .

Courtevue *(white with anger).* How dare you talk to me like this . . . I . . . why you're a disgrace to the Canadian episcopacy. *(He limps over to the door; he opens it and prepares to leave; he turns and addresses Charbonneau.)* I've had enough of your insolence and arrogance . . . I'm going to Rome to denounce you as a heretic . . . I . . .

Charbonneau *(waving).* Bonjour, Monseigneur Courtevue— *(Courtevue, showing disgust, exits. Charbonneau moves over to the window. He looks out on to the city. He shakes his head).* Lord. dear Lord, how can the Church help the people when even your bishops cannot agree on what is basic to man and to God? *(knocking at the door)* Yes . . . come in! *(Le Chef, fuming, bursts into the room. Charbonneau is startled.)* Well, well, another visit from the Prime Minister . . . what can I do for you?

Le Chef *(bluntly, dispensing with all courtesies and protocol).* Stop meddling in politics!

Charbonneau *(firmly).* It is my duty to tell the people what is Christian and what is not.

Le Chef. Your Excellency!

Charbonneau. Yes?

Le Chef. Christ said, "Give to Caesar the things that are Caesar's and to God the things that are God's." He did not tell Saint Peter or the Apostles to play around with politics.

Charbonneau *(solemn)*. When I seek justice for those who thirst after justice, I give to God the things that are God's.

Le Chef *(cynical, impatient)*. This is all very vague . . . What do you mean by justice?

Charbonneau. I mean this: Your decisions cannot flaunt the freedom and basic rights of the Asbestos strikers.

Le Chef *(angry)*. There are other rights besides those of the Asbestos strikers. And I warn you . . . I intend to oppose—indeed, I shall always oppose—any organization, union, or ecclesiastical, which, in my judgement, undermines the prosperity of our economy and hinders the industrialization of this backward province. What you fail to understand is that low wages attract to this province a great deal of needed American capital.

Charbonneau *(sharply)*. And that is why the foreigner refers to our workers as the Negroes of Canada. We provide the American investor with cheap and docile labour—

Le Chef *(impatient)*. Let me finish, Your Excellency . . . je vous en prie!

Charbonneau. I am listening.

Le Chef *(slowly with cold deliberation)*. I am Prime Minister of Quebec—le chef—I govern for all the people, for all the citizens, for the common good of all; not just for the well-being of the working class. I will do anything in my power to control, dominate, and even crush the Catholic unions when I think their demands are harmful to the common good and a hindrance to the prosperity of this province, I am going to—

Charbonneau *(interrupting)*. Excusez, Monsieur!

Le Chef *(impatient)*. Oui, Monseigneur?

Charbonneau *(with equal deliberation)*. I intend to give all my support to any organization, Catholic or not, which seeks justice for the working man.

Le Chef *(in a menacing tone)*. Prenez-garde, Monseigneur!

Charbonneau *(indignant)*. Take care, you say?

Le Chef *(waving a threatening finger in Charbonneau's face)*. I have all political power in my hands. I have an absolute majority in the legislature. I dominate my ministers like an absolute monarch. I can—

Charbonneau *(sarcastic)*. You can say, with Louis XIV, "L'état c'est moi!"

Le Chef *(sarcastic in his turn)*. Bien oui, Monseigneur . . . and I don't regard you as my Cardinal . . . Richelieu.

Charbonneau *(irritated)*. Sir!

Le Chef *(smiling thinly).* Qui?

Charbonneau *(walking over to his desk).* The Church does not exist to serve the government but to save the people. *(He picks a newspaper up from his desk.)* Do you read *Le Devoir?*

Le Chef *(startled).* Le Devoir, you mean the newspaper, *Le Devoir?*

Charbonneau. Exactly!

Le Chef *(petulant).* Not anymore,

Charbonneau. Why?

Le Chef. It's becoming a Communist rag, It falsifies the news on the strike, it attacks rightful authority, it cast aspersions on the laws, encourages sabotage and disorder, it is—

Charbonneau *(unfolding the newspaper in his hands).* Perhaps, perhaps, but have your read this editorial page *(He points to the paper.)* by Gerard Filion, concerning the strike?

Le Chef *(sternly).* Filion is a Communist.

Charbonneau *(He sits himself down at his desk; he looks up at the Prime Minister).* Sir, you call everyone a Communist who disagrees with your policies. Filion is a devout Catholic. What he writes here is certainly Catholic. He quotes Paul Claudel . . .

Le Chef *(impatient).* Damn it, Claudel is a poet, not a politician.

Charbonneau *(holding the newspaper in his hands, reading).* Allow me to read to you what Paul Claudel has to say about Christian charity. *(He reads out loud.)* "I want nothing to do with a Christian charity which is a constant capitulation of the spiritual to the temporal, I want nothing to do with a Christian charity which is a constant capitulation to kings and princes, to the rich and to monied interests, I want nothing to do with a Christian charity which is a constant abandonment of the poor and the oppressed, I recognize only one kind of Christian Charity; it is that charity which comes directly from Jesus: it is the constant communion, both spiritual and temporal, with the poor, the weak, and the oppressed . . . " *(Charbonneau stops reading, he looks up at the Prime Minister.)*

Le Chef *(with scorn).* That's a lot of silly poetry.

Charbonneau *(firmly).* It expresses my sentiments. For me, the Asbestos strikers are the poor, the weak, and the oppressed. They . . .

Le Chef. Nonsense. They are simply revolutionaries, They—

Charbonneau. Listen, please. Filion continues: "For many it is necessary that the poor remain poor, that's the rule. The poor, who try to escape from their poverty, are no longer poor, they are revolutionaries. We wish to give, but we do not wish to share. This egotistical form of giving alms attempts to use Christian charity in order to keep the poor poor, and to maintain social injustices. It has nothing to do with the gospel. We do not fight injustice with some kind of false charity, but with justice . . . " *(Charbonneau stops reading; he hands the paper over to the Prime Minister.)* Here, you read it!

Le Chef *(He takes the paper; he glances at the article for a few seconds).* Monseigneur, it is not the poets or the journalists who govern countries, but politicians like me. My entire political life and all my politics are inspired by a profound sense of justice and Christian charity. *(He appears angry.)*

Charbonneau *(still seated, fixing the Premier with a steady stare).* Monsieur le Ministre, I intend to read Filion's article at the next meeting of the Episcopal Commission.

Le Chef *(infuriated).* Then you persist in being a political meddler.

Charbonneau *(solemn).* I shall persist in a being a an Archbishop of the Church, not a bell-boy of the government. Our Catholic unions are defending the social teachings of the Church.

Le Chef *(threatening).* Excellency, beware! The unions rely more on the teachings of Communism than on the teachings of the Church . . . Besides I have enough power in my person to embarrass the Church.

Charbonneau *(growing angry).* Embarrass the Church? Just what do you mean?

Le Chef *(with slow deliberation).* If the Church continues to interfere in politics, I can fix her but good . . .

Charbonneau *(rising from his chair, almost shouting).* Is that a threat, sir?

Le Chef *(bending over the desk. Threatening, waving his finger in the Archbishop's face).* As Prime Minister of this province, and as Attorney-General, I can easily refuse grants and subsidies to your Catholic institutions. I can see to it that all Church properties are heavily taxed, I can—

Charbonneau *(shouting in anger).* This is insolence, sir; you are trying to blackmail me!

Le Chef *(smiling thinly).* Calm yourself, Monseigneur, calm yourself, I am simply prepared to use my political influence to prevent you from exercising your ecclesiastical influence improperly . . .

Charbonneau *(still shouting).* And I sir, am prepared to use my influence to protect the poor and the oppressed against the tyranny of your government . . .

Le Chef *(enraged).* You have been too easily influenced and swayed by the journalists of this damn newspaper, *Le Devoir.* *(He shakes the paper in his hands.)* You think and act like a Communist. I don't give a damn about this rag of a newspaper.

He tears it into little pieces, watching each piece fall to the floor. He kicks the pieces with his foot and stamps on them.

Charbonneau *(rising from his desk in anger, he rushes over to the Prime Minister. He faces him, his chin touching his nose).* You can't buy me, nobody can buy me .

Le Chef *(enraged)*. You're not the almighty one in the Church; I'll go to Rome and denounce you to the Pope; I'll tell him you're a Communist, I'll . . .

Charbonneau *(furious)*. Sir, be so good as to leave this room at once!

Le Chef *(He moves rapidly towards the door, like a fox on the run. The Archbishop pursues him like a lion.)* You just wait and see; I am more powerful than you think.

Charbonneau *(shouting at the top of his voice)*. Out, you hear, get out!

Le Chef. The Pope will fix you but good; he knows how to handle fools like you . . .

Le Chef slams the door as he leaves. Charbonneau is overcome with anguish and emotion. He clenches his fists, he bows his head against the wall near the door. He turns, he looks upwards, pleading; his lips move, murmuring a prayer; he walks over to his prie-Dieu. Exhausted, he falls to his knees; he hides his face in his hands; he begins to pray.

Charbonneau *(half sobbing)*. Lord God in heaven, hear my prayer, help me! I am sorry for my anger, please forgive my anger . . . my anger can harm the Church . . . forgive me . . . I'm proud and impulsive, help me now! *(He looks up at his crucifix.)* My burden is heavy . . . my life, as Archbishop, is a nightmare. My ideas are suspect, my administration criticized, my loyalty questioned . . . What am I to do? I must do what I think is right . . . Why did you choose me? Someone else—you should have chosen someone else for this archdiocese. Why me? I don't understand . . . I feel deep anguish of soul, I am alone, isolated from my colleagues . . . I . . . Oh, God, why didn't you leave me in Hearst. There, in Northern Ontario, I was happy, at home with the farmers and the new settlers. I am too inflexible for this giant diocese . . . too unfamiliar with the arts of diplomacy . . . I am too frank . . . too straight in my answers . . . God help me! Help me to make the right decisions for your Church, help me to act wisely, to govern prudently . . . and help me, Lord, to fight injustice . . . My heart is with the workers and miners of Asbestos . . . help me to help them . . .

De profundis claimavi ad te Domini,
Domini exaudi orationem meam.
Out of the depths I have cried to thee, O Lord, Lord hear my voice.
Let thy ears be attentive to the voice of my supplication.
If thou, O Lord, wilt mark iniquities: Lord who shall stand it.
For with thee there is merciful forgiveness:
And by reason of thy law I have waited for thee, O Lord.
From the morning watch even until night, let Israel be the hope in the Lord.
Because with the Lord there is mercy: and with him plentiful redemption.
And he shall redeem Israel from all his iniquities.

As he prays, music is heard in the background—the soft sad strains of a medley of French-Canadian folk songs. The lights dim, the statue of Maisonneuve casts a long shadow on the floor, snow splatters against the window pane, and the curtain falls.

Goin' Down the Road

William Fruet

Unpublished filmscript
First released 1970

Scenes 14, 15, 16
Characters in the excerpt: Peter, Joey, Old Man, Tramps, Street Crowds, Office Workers, Personnel Man, Secretary

Bill Fruet's screenplay was filmed in 1970 by a young Canadian director, Don Shebib. Fruet has since scored more writing success with the film *Wedding in White* which won the award for the best Canadian film of 1972.

Goin' Down the Road was a low budget ($82,000) picture, shot in 16mm. colour. It was distinguished for its clever blend of fiction and true-to-life documentary, a mixture which became in Shebib's hands an intensely sensitive kind of film realism. It was further distinguished by the meticulously convincing acting of Doug McGrath and Paul Bradley as the two youths, Peter and Joey. The movie was judged the best Canadian film of 1970.

Peter and Joey leave Nova Scotia to "make it" in the big city, but when they reach Toronto in their old Chevrolet convertible, they discover that instant success is not just around the corner. Their great expectations form a haze of naive fantasy and ignorant optimism in which the youths flounder not along the road, but down, down and down. Joey stumbles into a gauche marriage with a dull little waitress, while Peter dreams of jobs and girls he can never obtain. Debts are incurred, the pair steal food in a supermarket and make their escape by beating up the check-out clerk. Wanted by the police, they head for Vancouver.

The story of these messy young lives heading through vagrancy and petty crime to the gutters of skid row is made remarkable by the artists involved in the film. Although Peter might have fashioned something better from his life had he not seen himself as Joey's partner in losing, the film offers no easy solution for its hapless and incapable hero-victims. One is, instead, made to experience the problems of their type of life from their own confined viewpoint; it is a funny, bitter, frustrating dose, the taste of which cannot easily be forgotten.

Our three brief scenes from the movie call for as much from the supporting players as is demanded of Peter and Joey. The spectacle of these boys learning the harsh realities of the city against the background of Peter's grandiose schemes and stubborn, unwitting enthusiasm, is made convincing by small details, minute observation in the actors, and committed authenticity from the impersonal crowds. The crowd work could well be handled separately from the rest, and then the whole put carefully together for further rehearsal. These scenes provide, too, a good basis for improvisation.

Scene 14—Flophouse

Cut to sign of flophouse—"BED'S 75 CENTS PER NITE". Cut to Joey and Peter as they are led up a dimly lit hallway by a toothless old man in slippers and undershirt. They enter a dormitory crowded with rows of double bunks. There is the heavy odor of dirty feet and the sound of snoring everywhere. Peter pays the old man for two towels motioning to Joey. They put their gear down and slowly look over the setting. Several men are asleep, while others lie reading true detective magazines, etc. Several others are washing up, in a large washroom at the end of the hall.

Peter struggles to open the window. Joey sits on the bunk very depressed.

Joey *(scared).* Maybe we should head back huh?

Peter. We've got twenty-six dollars left. That isn't even gasoline to get us half way.

Joey. Whew! Does this place stink!

Peter. It ain't going to kill you for one night Joey . . . *(sits down on the bottom bunk and opens one of the newspapers they have bought)* . . . We just got to figure things out better that's all. No more hangups like today.

Joey. The place gives me the creeps.

Peter *(He stops and stares at the paper bewildered.)* What is this? There's hundreds of jobs in here! *(excited)* Look, look here, three pages of them.

Joey *(grabbing the other paper).* Let me see, let me see!

Peter. Listen to this . . . "Reservation agents—Textile salesman, Assistant manager, Sales trainees—We offer excellent promotional opportunities for the right man". Or listen to this! "Management trainee. Large advertising company has opening for young man interested in the advertising business". *(flops back on the bed, ecstatic with excitement)* Now this is more like it! It's right here. All you gotta do is go out and get it! What's wrong with that Hanson?

Joey. Hey, listen, to this. " '68 Plymouth Fury 2, auto, buckets, sharp! $1699.00 *(whistles)* Jeeze, that's about $400.00 less than you'd pay at home!

Peter *(cocky, confident).* Joey, I got it all figured! We'll check out a bunch of these jobs see! Take a look at things! Take our pick. Yeahhhh . . .

He lies back, lapsing into his own world of daydreams. Camera pans off them and across this strange selection of men who have taken shelter in a place like this for the night: men without roots, drifters and misfits.

Joey's voice. Hey you can even phone someone if you're lonely. Says right here! "Lonely? Telephone 923-1116."

Camera pans to the dirty window and the sleeping city outside.

Peter's voice *(dreamy).* You know, I wouldn't mind having a job in an office.

Joey's voice. What for? You'd have to get dressed up all the time.

Cut to the streets outside. Peter's words drifting over the big, towering buildings sitting silent and amused.

Peter's voice. Some chick for a secretary . . . company car . . . the whole bit. Why not?

Dissolve out.

Scene 15—Montage Jobs

Music comes up full and street comes alive with cars and activity of the morning rush hour, as everyone hurries to their place, their thing. Cut to Peter moving in the heavy crowded downtown streets. He wears a white shirt and tie and his hockey club windbreaker. Cut to Joey wandering along taking in the sights of the city. He comes upon a traffic jam. We cut to a sequence of Peter having several refusals in various offices. Music fades.

Scene 16—Advertising Agency

Cut to the frowning face of a personnel man who examines Peter's application form. His bewildered eyes keep coming up to Peter then darting back to the form. Finally he sits back and treats the situation with honesty and frankness.

Man. What ever possessed you to come here for a job? I mean looking at this I can't see anything in your background to even suggest an interest in advertising?

Peter. I used to watch a lot of commercials back home on television. *(trying to find words)* I mean I really enjoyed watching them. Like some of those car commercials. When the GTO comes up over the hill and you see it shooting along the desert . . .

Man. Obviously you've been influenced by them. But you must understand there's much more to it than that . . . *(looking down at the application)* You've been a "carpenter's apprentice", "painter", "six months with a cartage company".

Secretary enters, handing him papers to sign.

Man *(referring to the form again).* You haven't even finished high school. The kind of job you're applying for calls for a university degree.

Peter. Wasn't any point in finishing school. Do ya need an education to work in the mines? Or unload at the docks? There ain't a hell of a lot to pick from in the Maritimes you know!

The man signs some papers excuses himself and leaves Peter alone.

Fifteen Miles of Broken Glass

Thomas Hendry

Published 1972
Televised 1966, by C.B.C.

From Act I, Scene 4
Characters in the excerpt: Alec, Billy Stolz, Bud

Tom Hendry was born in 1929 in Winnipeg where he later became a co-founder of Theatre 77, and after that of the Manitoba Theatre Centre. From 1964-69 he was secretary-general of the Canadian Theatre Centre. He spent the following year at the Stratford Festival Theatre as literary manager. Besides directing in the theatre, Mr. Hendry has written for radio and television and various magazines. He is also a co-founder and president of the Toronto Free Theatre.

Fifteen Miles of Broken Glass won the Ontario Lieutenant-Governor's medal for 1970 as Best Canadian Play of the year. It was first produced for the stage in January 1971 by Central Players Theatre. The play is a vivid study of an adolescent trying to appear grown-up and manly by using the Second World War as a kind of private initiation into manhood. The war in Europe is over, but Alec's personal need for maturity, his naive, fanatical idea of heroism, and his love of the Air Force he is too young to join, insulate him from grim realities and make him hope that the Japanese will prolong the war until he can join up, complete his training and fly missions against them. His gauche efforts as a man who can handle a gun, as a would-be airman and as a lover all end in confusion and ridiculous defeat for him. They are all part of his clumsy efforts to be mature.

The excerpt here shows what happens when a war-weary young veteran returns home with the real war still clinging to him and is confronted by the already out-dated and impossibly romantic attitudes of Alec. An interesting feature of this excerpt is the setting in a pool hall, and the use of the pool table as a focus for stage business.

Alec and Stolz enter the pool hall. They have cokes in their hands.

Alec. Hey . . . who was that?

Billy. Looked like Buddy Haynes to me.

Alec. He's overseas isn't he? Didn't we send him a parcel for Easter, or something, from school?

Billy. That is Buddy Haynes, Alec, or I am a *Dutchman*.

Alec. Could be.

Billy. I'm telling you . . . it's Buddy Haynes . . . he's back . . . let's go talk to him.

Alec. What about?

Billy. This and that.

Alec. Aaaahhh, what are you going to say to a guy like that?

Billy. We'll ask him what it was like, combat, the war in the air, dicing with death, things like that.

Alec. Aaahhh, he'll treat us like a couple of kids.

Bud *(singing Old Lang Syne).* Who wants a game?

Alec. Well, all right. But don't blame me if we get the brush.

Billy. Hi there, Buddy. Nice to see you back safe and sound.

Bud. Yeah, sure. How's it going kiddo?

Billy. Oh, you know . . . how's it with you . . . when'd you get home?

Bud. Last night . . . look, I'm trying to shoot pool, do you mind?

Billy. Gee no, Bud . . . sorry to barge in . . . see you around.

Bud. Yeah, sure . . . see you around, eh?

Alec. You see what I mean . . . a guy like that has got important things on his mind . . . he doesn't want to waste his time talking to a bunch of kids.

Billy. I don't see why people have to go around biting a person's head off.

Alec. Listen . . . no telling what he's been through . . . he's got things to think about.

Billy. So have I, for Cripes' sake.

Alec. Buddy used to be such a nice guy.

Billy. Put a uniform on somebody, my old man says, he turns into a monster.

Alec. Nice patriotic statement . . . sounds like one of old man Costello's gems. You listen to him you come away thinking we should have fought the Liberals instead of the Germans.

Billy. Listen you have to get used to guys like him . . . they're the kind you always end up working for.

Alec. Not me kiddo, I've always had a feeling it's a short life and a merry one for me . . . guys get killed in the air force you know . . . there's a war on you know.

Billy. You really think that? That you'll be killed?

Alec. Sometimes . . . I just don't feel I was meant to live a long time.

Billy. Aahh, everybody feels that way sometimes.

Alec. I feel that way all the time.

Bud. Hey Alec . . . Hey, McNabb!

Alec. Yeah?

Bud. Hey I didn't recognize you at first . . . I saw your brother-in-law in London . . . Tuesday.

Alec. This Tuesday?

Bud. Two days ago . . . he should be home any day now.

Alec. Yeah . . . Peggy got a letter.

Billy. Did you fly home, Bud?

Bud. Your sister still as good-looking as ever?

Alec. Yeah, I suppose so.

Bud. You want me to let you in on the big game?

Alec. Thanks Buddy . . . come on Stolz. *(They get cues.)*

Bud. You want a smoke . . . here.

Alec. Thanks. Hey! . . . American cigarettes . . . How about *that!*

Bud. Yeah I picked up a couple of cartons at Gander on the way back.

Alec. You saw Lenny on Tuesday, imagine that Stolz.

Bud. Large as life in London, and twice as crazy, as usual . . . boy, he must have about two hundred pictures of your sister . . . he's a nut, that guy.

Alec. You get a chance to talk to him?

Bud. Well, I did and I didn't . . . I ran into him in a pub . . . we were both kinda corned . . . he was playing the piano for a singsong.

Alec. Did he say when he's getting here?

Bud. Everything's kinda fuzzy . . . this week I think . . . yeah this week.

Alec. Today or tomorrow.

Bud. It'll depend if he catches a flip back.

Alec. Imagine . . . this week.

Bud. By rights he should have to wait for a boat . . . but you know Lenny . . . he's got some kind of a deal going to get on a 'plane.

Billy. How do you *like* that, eh? They don't tell us about that kind of thing in cadets . . . everything in the air force sounds so official.

Bud. Ah, it's like anything else . . . if you're willing to turn on the charm and kiss the odd ass . . . it isn't so official . . . and Lenny knows all the ropes.

Billy. Nice shot Bud, . . . *(to Alec, aside)* Ask him about his experiences.

Alec. Are you kidding? He's plastered.

Billy. So what? So let us in on the big secret . . . are you getting out?

Bud. Nah . . . I go on instructing in a month.

Alec. Hey, maybe you'll wind up teaching us how to fly . . . we're joining up in November.

Bud. Why? Do you have to?

Billy. We want to.

Bud. Don't be crazy, the war's over.

Billy. Not in the Pacific, it's not.

Bud. Pacific won't take long . . . the Yanks don't want any help winning that one . . . they're bombing the hell out of the place now.

Alec. Blockbusters didn't make the Germans quit . . .

Bud. They sure as hell helped . . . whose shot is it?

Alec. Sorry.

Billy. Anyhow, tell us a little bit about it.

Bud. About what?

Billy. Tell us about the war.

Bud. Bloody waste of time.

Billy. Waste of time? We beat them, didn't we?

Bud. We beat the Jerries . . . but now the Russians are moving in everywhere . . . that'll be your worry.

Billy. Your shot, Bud . . . come on.

Bud. What do you want to hear about? The war in the air? The glamour of it all? Dicing with death? That kind of thing?

Alec. Listen, Bud, at Air Cadets, we saw movies of what you guys had to put up with . . . you don't have to talk about it.

Billy. Unless you want to.

Bud *(leaning on table).* I gotta puke.

Billy. This way, Bud . . . come on Bud.

Bud. No, I'm okay.

Billy. You want to get a cup of coffee or anything, Bud.

Bud. I'll be all right in a minute . . . Last big raid I was on . . . Dresden . . . never saw any Jerry fighters . . . didn't even see any flak . . . open city, y'see . . . just went in and burned the place down . . . Dresden.

Billy. That's war Bud.

Bud. What do you know about it big mouth? . . . You saw movies down at Cadets, eh? Well I saw movies too . . . Jerry newsreels of that raid . . . bodies stacked up like cordwood . . . we killed a hundred and fifty thousand . . . civilians, in two hours . . . that's damn near more people than we've got in this whole town . . . little kids . . . they had'em in rows . . . thanks to us . . . that's what you want to get into, eh?

Alec. It wasn't your fault, Bud.

Bud. That's right, it wasn't my fault . . . I was acting under orders . . . I had to . . . but you guys . . . you stupid little jerks . . . you don't have to . . . you want to . . . you stupid little jerks. *(following as they go)* YOU STUPID LITTLE JERKS!

Fortune and Men's Eyes
John Herbert

Published 1967
First production, New York, 1967, by Actor's Playhouse

From Act I, Scene 2
Characters in the excerpt: Mona, Smitty, Rocky

    John Herbert, born in Toronto in 1926, has held a variety of jobs besides his theatre work. His play draws upon his personal experience of prison in his youth. The first production of *Fortune and Men's Eyes* was by Mitchell Nestor, director with The Little Room, at the Actors' Playhouse, New York. A film version has since appeared. It is one of the most outspoken and powerful plays yet written by a Canadian.
    The setting is a prison. The action of the play occurs between mid-October and Christmas Eve and centres on Smitty, a youth serving a six month jail term. The Christmas message forms an ironic background to the very disturbing spectacle of Smitty irredeemably losing his soul and human decency in the brutish hell of the prison.
    Our excerpt shows the possibility that Smitty might survive, and perhaps salvage his life, making his "six months really tell". Mona, sensitive and relatively friendly, might have helped in this salvation. Rocky, a brutal thug, behaves with the mockery and viciousness that later is to hasten the corruptible Smitty along the route which, at the end of the play, leads to his bitter vow of revenge upon us all. The scene, set in the dormitory cell they all share, calls for a relaxed, almost snug atmosphere which must be established very quickly so that it can be swiftly undermined by the menace and ruthlessness of Rocky.

A Canadian reformatory, prep school for the penitentiary. The inmates are usually young, but there are often older prisoners, as indicated by the dialogue in places. We are primarily concerned here with four who are young, though they tell us others exist. The overwhelming majority of prisoners in a reformatory are in the late teens and early twenties. Those who are older have been convicted of offenses that do not carry a sentence large enough to warrant sending them to a penitentiary. The setting is a dormitory with four beds and two doorways. One door leads to the corridor, but we do not see it. There is a stone alcove, angled so that we get the impression of a short hall. We hear the guard's key open this unseen door whenever he or the four inmates enter or exit. The whole upstage wall is barred so that we look into the corridor where the guard and inmates pass in entrance and exit. Another doorway leads to the toilet and shower room.

As scene opens, Smitty and Mona are lying or sitting on their own cots, each reading his own book. Rocky can be heard off-stage, singing in the shower room. Queenie and the Guard are both absent.

Rocky *(singing).* Oh, they call me The Jungle King, The Jungle King . . . *(shouting)* Hey-y—Smitty!

Smitty. Yeah? *(continues reading)*

Rocky *(off-stage).* Roll me some smokes!

Smitty. Okay, okay. *(He moves, still reading, to Rocky's cot, where he finds package of tobacco, but no papers.)*

Rocky *(still off-stage and singing).* Oh, the Lion and the Monkey . . .

Smitty. What you got there, Jan? You must have had thirty takeouts in three weeks.

Mona. It's a book of poems.

Smitty. Any good?

Mona. Yes, but it's not exactly what I wanted.

Smitty. I've got something better; well, more useful, anyway. Come here; have a look.

Mona *(after crossing to join Smitty on Rocky's bed).* "Advanced Automobile Mechanics." Very practical!

Smitty. I'm a practical guy. You see, I figure I might not be able to get a job in an office, because—well—bonding, and all that. You know what I mean. Anyway, I worked evenings after school and all day Saturday in my fath—in a garage. I learned a lot about car motors, so I might as well put it to use. Mechanics are paid pretty good, you know.

Mona. That's wonderful, Smitty. This way, your time won't be wasted. You can make your six months really tell, and then after . . .

Rocky *(entering singing and combing his hair).* The Jungle King, the Jungle King . . . Say-y! Whadya call this here scene—squatters' rights? Let me tellya somethin'—quick! In good ol' Cabbage-town, there's a li'l joint where me gang hangs out; it's called the Kay Won Cafe. Guess who runs it?

Smitty. A Chinaman?

Rocky. Wrong! Charlie owns it, but Rocky runs it. A pretty-boy comes in there 'n' I don't like his face much—me boys wait fer 'im outside, an' grab aholt his arm 'n' legs, an' Rock, who's welterweight champ 'round there, changes the smart guy's kisser a li'l.

Smitty. You don't like your punching bag to swing too free. Your toughs have to hold him, eh?

Rocky. I do things *my* way. There's another spot, on the roughest corner in town, called Eddie's Poolroom. Now—guess who runs it?

Smitty. Eddie?

Rocky. Oh boy, do you learn slow! Same story. Eddie owns the shack, but ya kin bet yer sweet billiard cue The Rock says who's behin' the eight ball 'round there.

Mona *(rising from Rocky's bed).* All right, Rocky—I get the point.

Rocky. Ya better see it, Pinhead—or I'll give ya a fat eye t' wear. Now beat it!

Smitty. Leave him alone.

Rocky. Oh, you ain't talkin' t' me.

Smitty. Just don't touch him.

Rocky. Whadya think he is—precious—or somethin'?

Smitty. Lay off, that's all.

Rocky. How come ya talk t' me like that? Ain't I good t'ya, kid? Don't I getya cookies outa the kitchen? An' rubber t' chew, off Holy Face?

Smitty. You're so good to me—and I'm sick of it all.

Rocky. Now, now! That ain't a nice way t' talk, when I just bin fixin' it up wit Baldy t' git us in "D" Dorm. Ain't that whatya wanted all along?

Smitty. Let's not overdo this "togetherness."

Rocky. Sad—sad—sad! We-ell—I guess I'll just hafta 'range us a li'l extra gym, so's ya don't feel too neglected. The boys'll wanna meet ya before we move inta their Big Dorm. Tommorrow afternoon, Smitty? Get together wit de gang—just like at Eddie's or the Kay Won?

Smitty. No, Rocky—no!

Rocky. No what? No ketchup or no applesauce?

Smitty. No–no extra gym.

The Black Bonspiel of Wullie MacCrimmon

W.O. Mitchell

Published 1966
Televised 1962, on C.B.C. Playdate

From Act III
Characters in the excerpt: Wullie, Pipe-Fitting, Malleable

Born in 1914 in Weyburn, Saskatchewan, W.O. Mitchell grew up in the Canadian West. He studied at the Universities of Manitoba and Alberta, and has since worked as a teacher, as a deck-hand on a tramp steamer and as a writer. His work includes radio and television scripts, as well as short stories and novels. Noted as a humourist, he won the Leacock Medal for humour in 1962.

The Black Bonspiel, presented as part of the radio and television series *Jake and the Kid,* was written as a story in 1950 and later adapted for stage, radio and television performance. The devil appears in a small community of curling enthusiasts. He tempts Wullie into arranging a match with the team from hell. This fantastic situation gives plenty of opportunity for satire of the little community and its people.

The comedy of our scene unfolds through clever little touches of character revelation and the interplay of personalities. Wullie, ensconced in his shoe repair shop, explains the situation and persuades Malleable to join the game. The Scottish accents of the characters present an interesting and difficult challenge.

Interior: Wullie's shop.
Sound: Tinkle of bell above door.
Pipe-fitting is back again—at the door he peers anxiously, sees Wullie.

Pipe. You—you all right, Wullie?

Wullie. Aye-he. He's been gone an hour.

Pipe *(to the counter).* That's nice. *(sigh of relief)*

Wullie *(turning away to the shoes-to-be-repaired shelf).* And how's Mrs. Harrison's waste-and-overflow?

Pipe. Fine—just fine. *(heads for his chair)* Now. *(clears his throat)* You—uh—finished with you—with what you was doing?

Wullie *(at the shoes-to-be-repaired shelf. Picks up The Devil's curling-boots and idly turns them over in his hands).* Aye.

Pipe *(pause).* Dripping.

Wullie. Oh.

Pipe-fitting has his chin in his arms over the back of the tilted wooden chair.

Pipe. Wasn't nothin' had to be done. C'rossion. C'rossion would of taken care of her. *(looks speculatively over to Wullie)* Funny thing about plumbin'. Time. C'rossion. Take care of just about fifty per cent of your leaks. *(still marking time and waiting for Wullie to say something about the visitor)* Why—I seen *new* jobs—sprayin' at every joint—I seen 'em tighten up by themselves—without a wrench—*(long pause)* C'rossion.

Wullie stares down at The Devil's curling-boots in his hands.

Pipe. You—ah—what—maybe it's none of my business—but just what business did he have with you?

Wullie tosses curling-boots to the counter.

Curlin'-boots?

Wullie. This was not his first call—couple weeks ago. He left his curling-boots—custom made—wanted the soles mended. Dropped back a wee bit early to—ah—said he had a little business with May Whittaker.

Pipe *(relieved).* Oh. That all.

Wullie. Well—no—it isn't, Pipe-fitting. It isn't all. *(goes to the last—sits)* It—ah—it isn't all—at all. *(clears throat)* He's quite fussy about curling.

Pipe. Is he.

Wullie. Aye. Says they curl a fast knock-out game in Hell.

Pipe. Do they.

Wullie. Volcanic deposit—smooth—fast—I imagine it's a lot like this artificial ice.

Pipe. I guess she might be. Did—uh—did you an' him talk curlin'?

Wullie. We did.

Pipe. Them boots. Was that all he come in for—an' to talk curlin'?

Wullie. No. No. *(picks up cobbling-hammer, tacks—couple of taps on the boot in front of him)* He says he has not a particularly good third. He—he's looking for a good third for his rink. He likes my game.

Pipe. Uh-huh.

Wullie. So—it wasna just the curling-boots. He had a proposition to make me. *(pause)* I sort of liked it.

Pipe. Get into an aitch of a mess takin' the Devil up on a proposition, Wullie.

Wullie. Aye. This one involved a curling-match. *(pause to send out a feeler with Pipe-fitting)* His rink against ours. *(assessing Pipe's response)* Pipe-fitting—if you're willing, I'll be wanting you for a match this Sabbath evening.

Pipe-fitting slowly lowers his chair back—straightening up.

Pipe. Agin—agin?

Wullie. Against Old Cloutie and his rink from Hell.

Pipe *(we see only a momentary hesitation on Pipe's face).* Why—sure. *(He gets up from his chair.)* Look—I'll tell Malleable for you—let Cross-cut ride. I figure he'd keep goin' once he got started. That's the way to do her . . . *(He starts for the door—stops at the counter and looks back to Wullie.)* Kind of curious—see who he's got on his rink. You know—local folks. *(to the door, hand on the knob)* Take old man Dowling went West in 'thirty-two just after he diddled Mrs. Fowler out of that correction line half section . . .

Door opens—bell tinkling—Malleable enters.

Pipe. Oh—Malleable—I was just headed your way . . .

Malleable. 'Day, Pipe-fitting—Wullie.

Wullie. Malleable.

Pipe-fitting and Malleable come back to the counter.

Malleable. What you Indians been plottin' agin the whites today?

Pipe. Ah—*(clears throat—lays hand on Malleable's shoulder)* Ah—Wullie—me an' Wullie was just talkin' over a match—Sunday night.

Malleable. Sunday night. Ain't any Sunday curlin'. Reverend Pringle fixed that.

Pipe. That is just a little pick-up match, Malleable. *(Wullie has come up to the counter.)* Wullie here made the arrangements. Keepin' it quiet. *(pause)* You interested?

Malleable *(sliding a plug out of his pocket).* Sure. *(He opens his jack knife.)* Who's she agin?

Wullie. Old Cloutie.

Malleable *(has the plug between thumb and knife blade—cuts off corner, and as he looks up at Wullie he raises the segment between thumb and knife blade to his mouth).* Who?

Wullie. Old Cloutie.

Malleable *(getting the chew right).* Who's he?

Pipe *(with a look at Wullie).* You ought to know, Malleable. Old friend of yours.

Malleable's head is back—he is slowly and ruminatively chewing—trying to remem-

ber anybody of that name. *Decides not. Shakes head slowly. Stops chewing—considers a moment, then shakes head again.*

Malleable. I don't know anybody that name. Now there was a fellow—Coonie—Herb Coonie—lived in the Springbank district—he curled—I remember once in a green bonspiel back in . . .

Pipe. Cloutie. Old Nick . . .

Wullie. The Devil, Malleable.

Malleable *(goes on chewing a second—hitch in the rhythm).* Oh. *(takes up careful chewing again)* Him.

Wullie. We have a match on Sunday night—I—uh—I have an agreement with him. A great deal depends on who wins the match.

Malleable. Oh?

Wullie. It's up to you whether you curl or not. Doesn't concern you—however it turns out. Just me.

Malleable *(ceases chewing suddenly).* An' if we lose?

Wullie. If we lose—the Devil has one more MacCrimmon soul—I'd like to depend on you for third.

Malleable's mouth is ominously still as he considers the proposition.

Malleable. Why—*(one slow chew)* sure, Wullie,—*(two slow chews)* sure—*(back in gear and chewing naturally).*

Wullie. Thank you, Malleable.

Pipe. Now look, Malleable—about Cross-cut . . .

Malleable. Uh-uh. You tell Cross-cut, you tell Father O'Halloran. I wouldn't say nothin' to Cross-cut.

Wullie. Sunday night.

Malleable. Okay. Sunday night. *(pause)* Don't you worry none, Wullie.

Wullie *(picks up the curling-boots—looks down at them).* Aye-he. *(looks up)* We better get in a couple of practices.

Malleable and Pipe-fitting are at the opened door.

Malleable and **Pipe.** Okay, Wullie. *(They go out.)*

Music: Sneak in "Devil" theme background for:
Wullie at the counter with The Devil's curling-boots in his hands—sighs. Looks up and out. Down at boots again. Up.

Wullie *(with fervent feeling).* Stand fast, Craigellachie. *(pause)*

Music: Up full, then out.

And curl to beat hell!

Do You Remember One September Afternoon?

David Watmough

Published 1967

From Act I
Characters in the excerpt: Sarah, Mary-Elizabeth, Dumb Dora

David Watmough was born in Cornwall in 1932, but now lives in Vancouver. He has had radio plays performed on C.B.C. and has acted at the Lincoln Center in New York, and on television in Canada and in England. He is collecting some of his monodramas in two complementary volumes: *Pictures of a Dying Landscape,* which is about growing up in Cornwall during World War II, and *Pictures of a Living Landscape,* where the central theme is living in the present in the New World. Kanata Records of Toronto have released three of his monodramas on disc, and a further ten of them have been published in *Ashes for Easter.*

Do You Remember One September Afternoon? is a piece of twentieth century "Gothic" in so far as it is grotesque and macabre, exploiting madness for the purposes of horror. It is, though, more than this. It is a play concerned not only with madness, but with guilt and the past, that "dark backward and abysm of time", as Shakespeare put it.

In this excerpt from the first act, Dumb Dora, weak-minded and carrying a child's bucket and spade in a weird, overgrown garden, presents a fascinating acting challenge, a mute role which must elicit pathos as well as fascinated horror. All three women are elderly, and dressed in rags.

Place: A garden in a state of decay.

Sarah. It was *Her* party. Something to do with our new funds . . . I remember that bit quite clearly. We were hard up. The thought of new funds . . . well, that was very cheering. We was all in the mood for a party, I don't mind telling you. God, the time flies . . . must've been five years ago, that.

Mary-Elizabeth *(stubbornly persisting).* I can tell you everyone who was here, Sarah. As a matter of fact it was 1933 that it happened. Now it's . . .

Sarah *(creaking with forced laughter).* Now it's bloody Domes-day, so let's not bother about dates, eh? I think it's time Dumb Dora had her liquor ration. Look, she's panting for it!

Dumb Dora on her knees, is scrabbling harder at the ground. Dirt is flying in all directions. She is making horrible grunts as she scrabbles.

Mary-Elizabeth. She seems happy enough. Why not let her be? I do believe she thinks she's at the beach with us all again. Remember the beach, Sarah? And the sunshiny days? *(She is all dreary and reminiscent now, partly from the drink, but partly because this is a basic constituent of her nature.)*

Sarah. She should stop that digging. It's getting on me nerves as well as down me neck! Why don't she try somewhere else than just here?

Mary-Elizabeth *(gradually rising to her feet and moving slowly in pace with her memories. . . .)* There was the pony cart . . . three of us young Brides of Christ on either side. *She* always took the reins. Old Ruby was the mare, clip clopping down those lanes. She really was an old grey mare, just like the song.

Sarah *(made restless).* What are you going on about? Here, take a drink and for God's sake, close your face after it.

Mary-Elizabeth *(through her tears).* We're old and unloved. No one wants us. The hair has grown on our faces, we're dirty and ugly. Even . . . even *She* is cold towards us.

Sarah. You're talking crap now, if ever I heard it! *She* prefers us to all of them, I say! *(She gets up and starts to pace up and down, swaying heavily.)* We count and they don't. *She can afford* to make games with us because we're on *Her* side. Right now *She's* somewhere laughing like Mother Macree at us. We was always her favourite girls Mary Elizabeth, always. Things don't change . . . *She* don't change. It's only your stupid carrying-on which is upsetting around here . . . that, and their jealous minds forever trying to get her attention.

Mary-Elizabeth *(tears gone, her voice lowered).* I'm frightened. It's getting dark. It's always getting dark earlier and earlier. Nobody cares what happens to us.

Sarah *(thoughtfully).* We got to pay, of course, pay for all that has passed. There's all the retribution, don't forget . . . we don't escape the retribution.

Mary-Elizabeth. What torture are you unearthing for us? Sometimes I think you're going out of your mind.

Sarah. *Me* going out of *My* mind? Why even Dumb Dora here, doesn't carry on like you. It's Mad Mary more than Dumb Dora, that's what it is.

Mary-Elizabeth *(rushing to Sarah and tugging frantically at her arm).* There was the party, Sarah, the dreadful party. Is that what you meant?

Sarah *(pushing her off).* SHUT UP! Shut your mouth.

Mary-Elizabeth. Sister Felicity, Mary Magdalene, Sister Veronica and myself all played 'I Spy'. I chose the surf, which was just a faint line beyond the glare of the sand.

Sarah *(sitting back and burping, then closing her eyes).* That was the time *She* left us to arrange for tea at the store on top of the cove, wasn't it?

Mary-Elizabeth *(clapping her hands with delight).* Oh, Sister Sarah! You see you *do* remember. It was 1914 and the last of our Cornish holidays. After that we did bandages for all those years. Bandages for the men at the Front.

Sarah *(relentlessly).* By the time *She* came back it was too late. There was a row going on. Sister Gertrude said she had the biggest tits in the order, the little liar.

Mary-Elizabeth *(quickly).* A moments foolishness. We were all young. Vocations were unsure. In a jiffy *She* had us praying. There in the shade with the sound of the little waterfall at our backs. Ave Maria Gratia Plenum . . . *She* wasted no time.

Sarah *(wickedly).* But sister Gertrude sent us packing. She was a V.A.D. nurse by the end of that year and a whore for the boys on leave in three. The tits may have got big then but they certainly wasn't before. My turn for a swig. Give it to me. *(She grabs the bottle from Dumb Dora.)*

Mary-Elizabeth. You remember only ugliness, but I can still dream of paradise. It used to be paradise in those early times. The summers were always warmer. *She* was so kind. And everything was so neat and so shiny clean. Our habits were so spick and span. Nothing was the same after those years and years with all the filthy bandages, except her. *She* didn't change then. She taught us to sing so beautifully, and how to arrange flowers in the chapel. It wasn't until later that *She* seemed to get bored with us, impatient with our different little ways.

Sarah. You're a fool, Mary Elizabeth. Remember Lot's wife if you want to remember anything, you stupid old woman.

Mary-Elizabeth. Lot's wife, yourself! It's you who's turned to stone, Sarah. It's you who're always unkind and heartless to me. *(She begins to sob.)*

Mary-Elizabeth *(biting her clenched knuckles).* You brought it up, not me. And now I can't block it out. There's no escape . . . you've cut off our escape.

Sarah *(crossing to her, her arm raised threateningly).* Quiet, or I'll make you quiet!

Mary-Elizabeth. The memories . . . they won't leave me alone, Sarah!

Sarah strikes her and Mary-Elizabeth falls to the ground whimpering . . . All this time Dora has been digging, discarding the wooden spade for her bare hands. The sandy earth is spraying in all directions. The other two women stare at her.

Sarah. I thought I told you to stop that!

Mary-Elizabeth *(whimpering from the ground where she is prostrate on her stomach . . . peering into the hollow Dora has made).* Look Sister Sarah, look what she's found.

Sarah. Whiskey bottles, just the ones we hid after the party. Good. There's more than I thought.

Mary-Elizabeth. No, Sarah, there's something else. I can see part of it, she's . . . she's uncovering it.

Sarah *(disconcerted).* We got enough bottles. Dumb Dora, quit your scrabbling.

Mary-Elizabeth *(slithering on her belly to the brink of the pit . . . There is triumph in her horror).* With every handful it becomes clearer, Sarah. I can make out more and more of it.

Sarah *(now decidedly nervous)*. We must go inside. Listen, I can hear the bells for Vespers. *(Bells toll off stage.)*

Mary-Elizabeth *(as Dumb Dora works herself up into a frenzy of digging).* There's material, Sarah, cloth that has not yet rotted.

Sarah *(desperately)*. Inside, we shall process towards the flickering lights. *(She has turned away from the pit.)* The air will be hot with the smell of wax. Incense will swirl like fog about the six giant candles of the high altar . . .

Mary-Elizabeth *(in wonderment)*. All these years, all these winters . . . through the rain, the endless rain soaking through this soil.

Sarah. The Tabernacle door will be open . . . the soft white silk . . . the pure padded walls . . . the careful lifting up of the Host into the Monstrance . . .

Mary-Elizabeth. Dumb Dora is going to raise it up for us. The past she will bring into the light.

Sarah *(singing to the tune of Tantum Ego)*. Therefore we before Him bending . . . this great Sacrament revere.

Mary-Elizabeth. Sarah, our retarded Sister has moved away the bottles, swept away the shards of broken glass. In the bottom of the pit I can see . . .

Sarah *(her nerve breaking)*. NO! In Christ's name! Dora! Mary Elizabeth! Come away!

Mary-Elizabeth. I can see, I can see . . .

Sarah *(torn between fleeing and seeing)*. Come in! Come on in. *She* is waiting, calling.

Mary-Elizabeth *(standing up and speaking quietly)*. Yes, Sarah, we must go in. We must go in and tell her we love her and need her forgiveness.

Sarah *(relieved, grasping at straws)*. Yes, that's it, Mary-Elizabeth. We've just misunderstood one another, *She* and us, that is. The others are in there waiting to be friends, let's not keep them waiting, eh?

Swaying and holding each other up, Sarah and Mary-Elizabeth move towards the place that they entered. Dumb Dora climbs out of the pit she has dug and, bent double, ambles even more slowly after them. She is carrying something concealed in the folds of her rags . . .

Sarah *(turning around)*. Dumb Dora wants to come too, don't you, Dumb Dora? *(pauses . . . speaking quietly)* What . . . what's that she's got there? What's she carrying?

Mary-Elizabeth *(now, more matter of factly, she tugs at Sarah's arm and walks slowly on in front. In remarkably even, almost-flat tones, she says . . .)* Come on, Sarah. Dumb Dora has a baby now to nurse, she found it in the pit.

Sarah *(running forward and tugging at Mary-Elizabeth's sleeve)*. What is it? What is it she's got?

They are now strung out across the stage; Mary-Elizabeth is almost in the wings.

Mary-Elizabeth *(in a loud clear voice).* It's an arm, Sarah. An *arm.*

She walks off stage with Sarah just behind her . . . The lights dim rapidly . . .

Colours in the Dark

James Reaney

First published 1969
First production Stratford, Ontario, 1967.

From Act II, Scenes 8, 9
Characters in the excerpt: Button, Son, Sal, Mixed Crowd, Gramp

Colours in the Dark had its première at Stratford in 1967, directed by John Hirsch. It grew partly out of work done with young people at Reaney's Listeners' Workshop, and out of various other experiments and earlier plays. It is an interesting mixture of what Peter Brook might call "the poor theatre" (i.e. a basic theatre in which the actors rely on the effects they can gain from exploiting simply their own bodies and voices on a bare stage) and the use of technical gadgets such as projectors and a good deal of lighting equipment. Reaney wants his plays to express what he calls "the delight of listening to words, the delight in making up patterns (scribbling with your body/bodies) of movement for fun and in play." In a note for the original production, he explained that the play is "designed to give you that mosaic-all-things-happening-at-the-same-time-higgledy-piggledy feeling that rummaging through a play box can give you."

The excerpt here is a light-hearted satire on university life. A sceptical teacher is surrounded by exuberant students, and comes into conflict with fantasy as well as literal belief in the Bible. It is a good exercise in speech and in crowd reactions.

SCREEN: *Slides of University College and its gargoyles.*

Gramp *(with megaphone).* And on our left—the quaint old Gothic Victorian building, University College, University of Toronto. Outside it is trimmed with one thousand corbels carved in stone by a Bohemian stone carver. Inside it is decorated with one thousand corbels carved in wood by the same old gentleman and no two of them the same. His *chef d'oeuvre* is admittedly a fantastic wood gryphon at the bottom of the East Staircase.

Sally. I will come with you to a lecture. Perhaps it will
do me good. It's my day off and I'm not due at
Moody Hall until suppertime.

Son. What's your job, Sally?

Sally. I work in the kitchen at the college here.

Son. This is Dr. Button. Old Testament Studies. I usually
go to sleep on all the coats back here.

Sally. Old Testament Studies. What a treat!

They sit down with the rest of the company on the chairs which have been arranged as for a lecture room.

9. UNIVERSITY COLLEGE: THE LECTURE OF DR. BUTTON

Girls. Oh, Dr. Button. We came across this tremendous
article on Babylonian women in *Mademoiselle.*

Button. *(played by Gramp).* Go away!

Boys. Sir. A friend of mine and I have been working on the
possible influence of Chinese ideograms on
Babylonian cuneiform.

Button. No influence at all. You're too precocious. You know
what precocious means? It means—cooked too soon.
All black and burnt on the outside. All running and raw
doughy inside.

Boys & Girls. Oh, sir.

*SCREEN: Shows a series of philosophers,
teachers such as Frye and McLuhan.*

Button. My lecture for today—Herman Shultz. Finally, Gunkel J. Hempel. O. Einfeldt, A. Weiser, A. Bentger. Widengren's book falls into two parts Pfeiffer barely allows Ezra as an international person. Yahweh. Quite naturally I hope that no one in this room believes literally all that is in the Bible. The Holy Spirit cannot teach you French in two minutes. The sun has never stood still. Whales choke on oranges let alone fully developed prophets. Yahweh is someone the Israelites made up over a period years during their wanderings—very useful, but not really there. Originally Yahweh—Jehovah or God to some of you—was probably a volcano. A volcano in eruption. Do I meet with any opposition to these remarks? I like to have some sort of opposition. Let me sketch out the opposing positions. One of them might be that there is a holy creative force which binds the Universe together, inspires people to believe in something—after all a volcano is better than nothing. All wrong of course, but I'm surprised you back there asleep on all the coats haven't made your usual outburst.

Son. A flower is like a star.

Button. Oachghwkwk! A flower is not like a star! Nothing is
like anyone else. Anything else. You've got to get
over thinking things are like other things.

Son. Then if a flower is not like a star, and nothing is like anything else then—all the spring goes out of me. I used to take such pleasure in little things—images, stones, pebbles, leaves, grasses, sedges—the grass is like a pen, its nib filled with seed—but it all seems—lies. I can't go on. There seems no reason to go on living or thinking.

Button. Surely there are some basic drives that you don't have to get all tortured with thought about. Why after Mrs. Button has cooked me one of her excellent

dinners and we retire for an evening of endearments and jollity, there seems at
least one reason for going on. Have another such dinner, another such evening.

Son. Are people like each other then?

Button. I'm not like Mrs. Button. Otherwise we'd not have
so much fun.

Class laughter.

Son *(advancing as if to assassinate).* A flower is like a star!

Button *(advancing too as in a menacing Kabuki scene).*
Don't come at me like that. A flower is not like
a star!

Son. You're a bear whose paw is over my sun.

Button. You've served my purpose. Class—that's the
imaginative point of view. Give it a big hand,
before it falls asleep on your coats again.

Applause.

Son. Don't you believe in anything?

Button *(pause).* Not a thing. Ever since Fritz Schmidlap was caught
planting 12th century sherds in a 9th century dig.
Imagine the idiocy of believing anything in the Old
Testament. Why there's a girl works in our college
kitchens who's not only copying out the whole Bible
into Woolworth's scribblers, but believes literally
every word it says.

Sal *(rising).* Sir—I am that girl. And I believe in God—or
Yahweh as you call him. And I believe every word
I possibly can of the book he wrote.

Button. *(dry laugh).* I suppose you think he wrote it in English.

Sal. He knows English for I have prayed to him in that
language and he has answered me.

Button. In English?

Sal *(pause).* How well do you know your Bible—in English, sir?

Button. Very well indeed. Last year I was elected President
of the Oriental Institute. I am a linguist of no
mean renown and world authority on Ugaritic ostraca.

Sal. Exodus, Chapter 34, verse 14, says?

Button. For thou shalt worship no other god: for the Lord,

whose name is Jealous, is a Jealous God. Kings II,
Chapter 9, verse 33?

Sal. And he said, Throw her down. So they threw her down
and some of her blood was sprinkled on the wall and
on the horses: and he trode her under foot. Kings II,
Chapter 10, verse 26 says?

Button. And they brought forth the images out of the house of
Baal and burned them. You believe no doubt in the
Holy Spirit. Yes?

Sal. Yes.

Button. And that he or it can give you the power to speak
with tongues?

Sal. Yes. I believe.

Button. Do you, in fact, know any other language but your
mother tongue?

She shakes her head.

I thought not. Anyone here know German, Hungarian,
French. Yes?

As hands are raised.

You precocious youngsters. I will also test her out
in Ancient Babylonian. Ready? I will ask you a
question in a foreign tongue. The Holy Spirit will
give you the power no doubt to reply to me in that
tongue.

Sal *(shutting her eyes)*. I pray that he will.

All. French!

Button. Moi et toi, ces seuls noms dans mon invocation?

From Claudel's version of Electra.

Sal *(hesitantly, then more and more smoothly)*. C'est à toi de comprendre et de
considérer.

All *(cheering)*. German!

Button. Wo hinaus so früh, Rothkäppchen?

From Grimm's "Red Riding Hood".

Sal. Zur Grossmutter.

The little girl's lines.

Button. Was tragst du unter der Schurze?

The wolf's lines.

Sal *(lit now in a blaze of glory).* Kuchen und Wein: gestern haben wir gebachen, da soll
sich die Kranke unser schwache Grossmutter etwas zu
gut tun, und sich damit starken!

All. Hungarian!

Button. Hungarian yourself! Ancient Babylonian. I'll get you
and your Holy Ghost there. No Berlitz School can teach
an ignorant kitchen slave Ancient Babylonian.

All. Ancient Babylonian!

We've let the typewriter wander over the first words of the Bible.

Button. Bresith bara elohim eth kassamayim weth haarec.

Sal. Whaarec hayatha tho hu wabbobu whoselch appne thehim.
Weruah marahepheth hammayim wayymen yehi or YEHI or
WAYEHI WAYEHI

*BUTTON exits in shame and wrath.
Underneath the love scene Father and Mother
chant other metaphor equations: flower star
deer branch tree antler antler branch clock
heart eye sun mouth bell cloud Greenland*

All.   A flower is
                     like a star!
                     A flower is like a star!
                     A flower is like a star!

SCREEN: Star—flower—butterfly—montage.

Son. No, no. Try this. A flower is a star.

All *(chatting in the background).* A flower is a star. A flower is a star.

Son and Sal walk towards each other.

SCREEN: Green leaf. By this time thy SON and SAL should be standing on chairs.

Sal. Do you remember that great big leaf we found on the island?

*Sing this à la Les Parapluies de Cherbourg. Let the actors and pianist make up their
own tunes.*

Son. Yes. Adam and Eve could have hidden all their shame in it.

Sal. Have you pressed it for me in the heaviest book in the
library?

Son. I did. But someone took out the heaviest book. I can't find out who.

Sal. *(spoken).* What a shame! If you had been able to give me the green or a luna moth leaf . . .

Son. Teach me how to believe the way you do.

Sal. My darling . . . isn't it simply that *(she presents herself to him, but he turns away)* no one can teach it to you. It teaches you—to itself *(an embrace in which he is backward to her).*
But instead I'll finish copying out the whole Bible.
Tonight—I'll begin the New Testament. I have the strength at last to write of Jesus.

Leaving Home

David French

Published 1972
First production Toronto, 1972, by Tarragon Theatre

From Act I
Characters in the excerpt: Mary, Bill, Ben

David French was born in 1939 in Newfoundland. When he was six the family moved to Toronto. He has been writing since his teens and sold his first television play when he was twenty-three. He has studied at the Pasadena Playhouse in California, and in Toronto and New York. He has written scripts for C.B.C. Television.

Leaving Home opened on 16 May, 1972 at the Tarragon Theatre in an accomplished and successful production later shown on television. Other stage productions followed with unusual rapidity in Halifax, Montreal and Edmonton. The play is set in Mary and Jacob Mercer's working-class home in Toronto, early in November, sometime in the late 1950's. The action is continuous and the play obeys the unities of time and place. There are two threads to the action. There is the clumsy, pathetic relationship Bill has with his girl, Kathy, with their half-hearted plans for marriage and independence. And there is the break from the turbulent Mercer home made by Ben, the clever, more studious son. The characters fall into a pattern reminiscent of those we find in D.H. Lawrence's *Sons and Lovers:* a lonely, bitter, and quarrelsome father who at times is vital and well-meaning, but is mastered by his temper and his pride, and so remains isolated and frustrated; a gentler, sympathetic, strong mother, whose life has become son-centred; the sons on the verge of manhood, each approaching it in his different way, with the more intellectual son challenging the father.

Our excerpt is the opening of the play, with its moment of relative calm, unobtrusive exposition and family chatter before the appearance of the troublesome Jacob. One is reminded at times of the compassionate view of ordinary people in the realistic plays of Sean O'Casey. Mary and Jacob owe something to their great precedents, O'Casey's Juno and her Paycock.

The lights come up on a working-class house in Toronto. The stage is divided into three playing areas: kitchen, dining room, and living room. In addition there is a hallway leading into the living room. Two bedroom doors lead off the hallway, as well as the front door which is offstage.

The kitchen contains a fridge, a stove, cupboards over the sink for everyday dishes, and a small drop-leaf table with two wooden chairs, one at either end. A plastic garbage receptacle stands beside the stove. A hockey calendar hangs on a wall, and a kitchen prayer.

The dining room is furnished simply with an oak table and chairs. There is an oak cabinet containing the good dishes and silverware. Perhaps a family portrait hangs on the wall—a photo taken when the sons were much younger.

The living room contains a chesterfield and an armchair, a T.V., a record player and a fireplace. On the mantle rests a photo album and a silver-framed photo of the two sons—then small boys—astride a pinto pony. On one wall hangs a mirror. On another, a seascape. There is also a small table with a telephone on it.

It is around five-thirty on a Friday afternoon, and Mary Mercer, aged fifty, stands before the mirror in the living room, admiring her brand new dress and fixed hair. As she preens, the front door opens and in walk her two sons, Ben, eighteen, and Bill, seventeen. Each carries a box from a formal rental shop and schoolbooks.

Mary. Did you bump into your father?

Ben. No, we just missed him, Mom. He's already picked up his tux. He's probably at the Oakwood. *(He opens the fridge and helps himself to a beer.)*

Mary. Get your big nose out of the fridge. And put down that beer. You'll spoil your appetite.

Ben. No, I won't. *(He searches for a bottle opener in a drawer.)*

Mary. And don't contradict me. What other bad habits you learned lately?

Ben *(teasing).* Don't be such a grouch. You sound like Dad. *(He sits at the table and opens his beer.)*

Mary. Yes, well just because you're in university now, don't t'ink you can raid the fridge any time you likes.

Bill crosses the kitchen and throws his black binder and books in the garbage receptacle.

Mary. What's that for? *(Bill exits into his bedroom and she calls after him.)* It's not the end of the world, my son. *(pause)* Tell you the truth, Ben. We always figured you'd be the one to land in trouble, if anyone did. I don't mean that as an insult. You're more . . . I don't know . . . like your father.

Ben. I am?

Music from Bill's room.

Mary *(calling, exasperated).* Billy, do you have to have that so loud? *(Bill turns down his record player. To Ben)* I'm glad your graduation went okay last night. How was Billy? Was he glad he went?

Ben. Well, he wasn't upset, if that's what you mean.

Mary *(slight pause).* Ben, how come you not to ask your father?

Ben. What do you mean?

Bill *(off).* Mom, will you pack my suitcase? I can't get everything in.

Mary *(calling).* I can't now, Billy. Later.

Ben. I want to talk to you, Mom. It's important.

Mary. I want to talk to you, too.

Bill *(comes out of bedroom, crosses to kitchen).* Mom, here's the deposit on my locker. I cleaned it out and threw away all my old gym clothes. *(He helps himself to an apple from the fridge.)*

Mary. Didn't you just hear me tell your brother to stay out of there? I might as well talk to the sink. Well, you can t'row away your old school clothes—that's your affair—but take those books out of the garbage. Go on. You never knows. They might come in handy sometime.

Bill. How? *(He takes the books out, then sits at the table with Ben.)*

Mary. Well, you can always go to night school and get your senior matric, once the baby arrives and Kathy's back to work . . . Poor child. I talked to her on the phone this morning. She's still upset, and I don't blame her. I'd be hurt myself if my own mother was too drunk to show up for my shower.

Bill *(a slight ray of hope).* Maybe she won't show up tonight.

Mary *(glances anxiously at the kitchen clock and turns to check the fish and potatoes).* Look at the time, I just wish to goodness he had more t'ought, your father. The supper'll dry up if he don't hurry. He might pick up a phone and mention when he'll be home. Not a grain of t'ought in his head. And I wouldn't put it past him to forget his tux in the beer parlour. *(Finally she turns and looks at her two sons, disappointed.)* And look at the two of you. Too busy with your mouths to give your mother a second glance. I could stand here till my legs dropped off before either of you would notice my dress.

Ben. It's beautiful, Mom.

Mary. That the truth?

Bill. Would we lie to you, Mom?

Mary. Just so long as I don't look foolish next to Minnie. She can afford to dress up—Willard left her well off when he died.

Ben. Don't worry about the money. Dad won't mind.

Mary. Well, it's not every day your own son gets married, is it? *(to Bill as she puts on large apron)* It's just that I don't want Minnie Jackson looking all decked out like the *Queen Mary* and me the tug that dragged her in. You understands, don't you, Ben?

Ben. Sure.

Bill. I understand too, Mom.

Mary. I know you do, Billy. I know you do. *(She opens a tin of peaches and fills* *five dessert dishes.)* Minnie used to go with your father. Did you know that, Billy? Years and years ago.

Bill. No kidding?

Ben *(at the same time).* Really?

Mary. True as God is in Heaven. Minnie was awful sweet on Dad, too. She t'ought the world of him.

Bill *(incredulously).* Dad?

Mary. Don't act so surprised. Your father was quite a one with the girls.

Ben. No kidding?

Mary. He could have had his pick of any number of girls. *(to Bill)* You ask Minnie sometime. Of course, in those days I was going with Jerome McKenzie, who later became a Queen's Counsel in St. John's. I must have mentioned him.

The boys exchange smiles.

Ben. I think you have, Mom.

Bill. A hundred times.

Mary *(gently indignant—to Bill).* And that I haven't!

Bill. She has too. Hasn't she, Ben?

Mary. Never you mind, Ben. *(to Bill)* And instead of sitting around gabbing so much you'd better go change your clothes. Kathy'll soon be here. *(as Bill crosses to his bedroom)* Is the rehearsal still at eight?

Bill. We're supposed to meet Father Douglas at the church at five to. I just hope Dad's not too drunk. *(He exits.)*

Mary *(studies Ben a moment).* Look at yourself. A cigarette in one hand, a bottle of beer in the other, at your age! You didn't learn any of your bad habits from me, I can tell you. *(pause)* Ben, don't be in such a hurry to grow up. *(She sits across from him.)* Whatever you do, don't be in such a hurry. Look at your poor young brother. His whole life ruined. Oh, I could weep a bellyful when I t'inks of it. Just seventeen, not old enough to sprout whiskers on his chin, and already the burdens of a man on his t'in little shoulders. Your poor father hasn't slept a full night since this happened. Did you know that? He had such high hopes for Billy. He wanted you both to go to college and not have to work as hard as he's had to all his life. And now look. You have more sense than that, Ben. Don't let life trap you.

Bill enters. He has changed his pants and is buttoning a clean white shirt. Mary goes into the dining room and begins to remove the tablecloth from the dining room table.

Bill. Mom, what about Dad? He won't start picking on the priest, will he? You know how he likes to argue.

Mary. He won't say a word, my son. You needn't worry. Worry more about Minnie showing up.

Bill. What if he's drunk?

Mary. He won't be. Your father knows better than to sound off in church. Oh, and another t'ing—he wants you to polish his shoes for tonight. They're in the bedroom. The polish is on your dresser. You needn't be too fussy.

Ben. I'll do his shoes, Mom. Billy's all dressed.

Mary. No, no, Ben, that's all right. He asked Billy to.

Bill. What did Ben do this time?

Mary. He didn't do anyt'ing.

Bill. He must have.

Mary. Is it too much trouble to polish your father's shoes, after all he does for you? If you won't do it, I'll do it myself.

Bill *(indignantly).* How come when Dad's mad at Ben, I get all the dirty jobs? Jeez! Will I be glad to get out of here! *(Rolling up his shirt sleeves he exits into his bedroom.)*

Mary takes a clean white linen tablecloth from a drawer in the cabinet and covers the table. During the following scene she sets five places with her good glasses, silverware and plates.

Ben *(slight pause).* Billy's right, isn't he? What'd I do, Mom?

Mary. Take it up with your father. I'm tired of being the middle man.

Ben. Is it because of last night? *(slight pause)* It is, isn't it?

Mary. He t'inks you didn't want him there, Ben. He t'inks you're ashamed of him.

Ben. He wouldn't have gone, Mom. That's the only reason I never invited him.

Mary. He would have went, last night.

Ben *(angrily).* He's never even been to one lousy Parents' Night in thirteen years. Not one! And he calls *me* contrary!

Mary. You listen to me. Your father never got past Grade T'ree. He was yanked out of school and made to work. In those days, back home, he was lucky to get that much and don't kid yourself.

Ben. Yeah? So?

Mary. So? So he's afraid to. He's afraid of sticking out. Is that so hard to understand? Is it?

Ben. What're you getting angry about? All I said was—

Mary. You say he don't take an interest, but he was proud enough to show off your report cards all those years. I suppose with you that don't count for much.

Ben. All right. But he never goes anywhere without you, Mom, and last night you were here at the shower.

Mary. Last night was different, Ben, and you ought to know that. It was your high school graduation. He would have went with me or without me. If you'd only asked him.

A truck horn blasts twice.

There he is now in the driveway. Whatever happens, don't fall for his old tricks. He'll be looking for a fight, and doing his best to find any excuse. *(calling)* Billy, you hear that? Don't complain about the shoes, once your father comes!

Ben *(urgently).* Mom, there's something I want to tell you before Dad comes in.

Mary. Sure, my son. Go ahead. I'm listening. What's on your mind?

Ben. Well . . .

Mary *(smiling).* Come on. It can't be that bad.

Ben *(slight pause).* I want to move out, Mom.

Mary *(almost inaudibly).* What?

Ben. I said I want to move out.

Mary *(softly, as she sets the cutlery).* I heard you. *(pause)* What for?

Ben. I just think it's time. I'll be nineteen soon. *(pause)* I'm moving in with Billy and Kathy and help pay the rent. *(pause)* I won't be far away. I'll see you on weekends. *(Mary nods)* Mom?

Mary *(absently).* What?

Ben. Will you tell Dad? *(slight pause)* Mom? Did you hear me?

Mary. I heard you. He'll be upset, I can tell you. By rights you ought to tell him yourself.

Ben. If I do, we'll just get in a big fight and you know it. He'll take it better, coming from you.

The Ecstasy of Rita Joe

George Ryga

Published in 1971
First production 1967, by Vancouver Playhouse.

From Act I
Characters in the excerpt: Rita Joe, Magistrate, Policeman, Eileen, Old Woman, Jaimie, Four Murderers.

    George Ryga, born in 1932, grew up on a farm in Alberta and is largely self-educated. He has studied, done a variety of jobs, including radio work, and since 1962 has devoted himself to being a professional writer. His work includes poetry, short stories, novels, filmscripts and plays for stage and television.
    The Ecstasy of Rita Joe, first performed on 23 November, 1967 in Vancouver Playhouse, has since been seen in an extremely successful ballet version danced by the Royal Winnipeg Ballet. Brian Parker, in his edition of stage plays by Ryga (New Press, 1971) describes them as peasant tragedy, noting comparisons with the plays of the Spanish writer, Lorca. Parker also draws attention to Ryga's use of such ballad techniques as the tendency to switch from one significant incident to another without preamble, focussing only on selected moments in the narrative. While Ryga's work is as yet uneven, and lacks the stature achieved by Lorca's, his stage techniques are extremely interesting. By means of multi-purpose sets and versatile lighting effects, Ryga is able to stage incidents from both the present and the past simultaneously, switching freely in time and place by lighting up actions in different parts of the stage. In this way he can lead us inside a character's mind and reveal to us that the landscape of the present co-exists with the country of the past. At its best, the dream-like effect of the play is no mere arty evasion of the realities of an Indian way of life in modern Canada, for the dream is in fact the nightmare of being an Indian, disinherited in one's own country, and caught in the legal grip of an alien society with a foreign code of conscience. Rita Joe is an Indian woman whose life of vagrancy, petty crime and police courts becomes representative of the difficulties and misfortunes of her people.
    The excerpt here shows Rita Joe in court, stubbornly keeping to her own ways, preserving a fragile integrity totally at odds with the well-meaning but institutionalized figure of the magistrate. The lacrosse game (invented of course by Indians) externalizes a fleeting fragment from Rita Joe's memory as she stands in court. It is also a fine exercise in group mime and timing, which must, by its tempo and patterns of gesture, help to intensify the dialogue and situation.

A circular ramp—beginning at floor level stage left and continuing downward below floor level at stage front, then rising and sweeping along stage back at two-foot elevation to disappear in wings of stage left. This ramp dominates the stage by wrapping the central and forward playing area. A short approach ramp, meeting with the main ramp at stage right, expedites entrances from wings of stage right.

The Magistrate's chair and representation of court desk are situated at stage right, enclosed within the sweep of the ramp. At the foot of the desk is a lip on stage right side. The Singer sits here, turned away from the focus of the play. Her songs and accompaniment appear almost accidental. She has all the reactions of a white liberal folklorist with a limited concern and understanding of an ethnic dilemma which she touches in the course of her research and work in compiling and writing folk songs. She serves, too, as an alter ego to Rita.

No curtain is used during the play. At the opening, intermission and conclusion of the play, the curtain remains up. Because of this, the onus for isolating scenes from the past and present in Rita Joe's life falls on highlight lighting.

Backstage, a mountain cyclorama is lowered into place. In front of the cyclorama, a darker maze curtain to suggest gloom and confusion, and a cityscape.

House lights and stage work lights remain on. Backstage, cyclorama, and maze curtain are up, revealing wall back of stage, exit doors, etc.

Cast, Singer enter off stage singly and in pairs from wings, exit doors back of theatre, from auditorium side doors. The entrances are workmanlike and untheatrical. When all the cast is on stage, they turn to face the audience momentarily. House lights dim.

Cyclorama lowers into place. Maze curtain follows. This creates a sense of compression of stage into the auditorium. Recorded voices are heard in a jumble of mutterings and throat clearings.

The Policeman grabs and shakes Rita Joe to snap her out of her reverie. Light on Magistrate, who sits erect, with authority.

Magistrate. I ask you for the last time, Rita Joe . . . do you want a lawyer?

Rita *(defiant).* What for? . . . I can take care of myself.

Magistrate. The charge against you this morning is prostitution. Why did you not return to your people as you said you would?

Light on back stage dies. Rita Joe stands before Magistrate and policeman. She is contained in a pool of light before them.

Rita *(nervous, with despair).* I tried . . . I tried . . .

The magistrate settles back into his chair and takes folder from his desk which he opens and studies.

Magistrate. Special Constable Eric Wilson has submitted a statement to the effect that on June 18th he and Special Constable Schneider approached you on Fourth Avenue at nine-forty in the evening . . .

Policeman. We were impersonating two deck-hands newly arrived in the city . . .

Magistrate. You were arrested an hour later on charges of prostitution.

The magistrate holds the folder threateningly and looks down at her. Rita Joe is defiant.

Rita. That's a goddamned lie!

Magistrate *(sternly, gesturing to Policeman).* This is a police statement. Surely you don't think a mistake was made?

Rita *(peering into the light above her, shuddering).* Everything in this room is like ice . . . How can you stay alive working here? . . . I'm so hungry I want to throw up . . .

Magistrate. You have heard the statement, Rita Joe . . . Do you deny it?

Rita. I was going home, trying to find the highway . . . I knew those two were cops the moment I saw them . . . I told them to go f . . . fly a kite! They got sore then an' started pushing me around . . .

Magistrate *(patiently now, waving down objections of the policeman).* Go on.

Rita. They followed me around until a third cop drove up. An' then they arrested me.

Magistrate. Arrested you . . . nothing else?

Rita. They stuffed five dollar bills in my pockets when they had me in the car . . . I ask you, mister, when are they gonna charge cops like that with contributing to delinquency?

Policeman. Your Worship . . .

Magistrate *(irritably, indicating folder on the table before him).* Now it's your word against this! You need references . . . people who know you . . . who will come to court to substantiate what you say—today! That is the process of legal argument!

Rita. Can I bum a cigarette someplace?

Magistrate. No. You can't smoke in court.

Policeman smiles and exits.

Rita. Then give me a bed to sleep on, or is the sun gonna rise an' rise until it burns a hole in my head?

Guitar music cues softly in background.

Magistrate. Tell me about the child.

Rita. What child?

Magistrate. The little girl I once saw beside the road!

Rita. I don't know any girl, mister! When do I eat? Why does an Indian wait even when he's there first thing in the morning?

Pool of light tightens around Magistrate and Rita Joe. Separate light on riser ramp backstage isolates Indian boys and Jaimie. Rita Joe's attention strays to mental awareness of them. They are playing a lacrosse game in slow motion.

Magistrate. I have children . . . two sons . . .

Rita *(nods).* Sure. That's good.

The magistrate gropes for words to express a message that is very precious to him.

Magistrate. My sons can go in any direction they wish . . . into trades or university . . . But if I had a daughter, I would be more concerned . . .

Rita. What's so special about a girl?

Magistrate. I would wish . . . well, I'd be concerned about her choices . . . her choices of a living, school . . . friends . . . These things don't come as lightly for a girl. For boys it is different . . . *(The "lacrosse game" freezes in silhouette.)* But I would worry if I had a daughter . . . Don't hide your child! Someone else can be found to raise her if you can't! *(Rita Joe shakes her head, strange smile on her face.)* Why not? There are people who would love to take care of it.

Rita. Nobody would get my child . . . I would sooner kill it an' bury it first! I am not a kind woman, mister judge!

Magistrate *(at a loss).* I see . . .

Rita *(a cry).* I want to go home . . .

Quick up tempo music, and lights change suddenly. Lacrosse game picks up tempo, again at normal speed. Jaimie and the Indian Boys sweep over the entire ramp, the light widening for them. Rita Joe follows them in their game, turning from one man to another until she sees Jaimie. Eileen and old woman enter.

Rita. Jaimie!

Eileen *(happily, running to him).* Jaimie Paul! God's sakes . . . when did you get back from the north? . . . I thought you said you wasn't coming until break-up . . .

The game has turned into a railway station crowd on a platform. Jaimie turns to Eileen.

Jaimie. I was comin' home on the train . . . had a bit to drink and was feeling pretty good . . . lots of women sleeping in their seats on the train . . . I'd lift their hats an' say, "Excuse me, lady . . . I'm lookin' for a wife!" *(turns to old woman)* One fat lady got mad, an' I says to her—"That's all right, lady . . . you got no worries . . . you keep sleepin'!" *(laughter)*

Jaimie and old woman move away. Eileen sees Rita standing watching.

Eileen. Rita! . . . Tom an' I broke up . . . did I tell you?

Rita. No, Leenie—you didn't tell me!

Eileen. He was no good . . . he stopped comin' to see me when he said he would. I kept waiting, but he didn't come . . .

Rita. I sent you a pillow for your wedding!

Eileen. I gave it away . . . I gave it to Clara Hill.

Rita *(laughs bawdily and mimes pregnancy).* Clara Hill don't need no pillow now!

Jaimie *(smiling, crosses by her and exiting).* I always came to see you, Rita Joe . . .

Rita looks bewildered.

Old Woman *(exiting).* I made two Saskatoon pies. Rita . . . you said next time you came home you wanted Saskatoon pie with lots of sugar . . .

Eileen and Old Woman drift away. Jaimie Paul moves on to shadows. The Three Murderers enter in silhouette; one whistles. Rita rushes to the young indians in stage front.

Rita. This is me, Rita Joe, God's sakes . . . We went to the same school together—don't you know me now—Johnny? You remember how tough you was when you was a boy? . . . We tied you up in the Rainbow Creek and forgot you was there after recess . . . An' after school was out, somebody remembered . . . *(She laughs.)* And you was blue when we got to you. Your clothes was wet to the chin, an' you said, "That's a pretty good knot—I almost give up trying to untie it!"

The music continues. Rita steps amongst the Boys and they mime being piled in a car at a drive-in.

Rita. Steve Laporte? . . . You remember us goin' to the drive-in and the cold rain comin' down the car windows so we couldn't see the picture show anyhow?

She sits beside Steve Laporte. They mime the windshield wipers. A cold white light comes up on playing area directly in front of Magistrate's chair. A young man of disheveled, dirty appearance steps into light and delivers testimony in a whining, defensive voice. He is one of the Murderers, but apart from the other three, he is nervous.

Young Man. I gave her three bucks . . . an' once I got her goin' she started yellin' like hell! Called me a dog, pig . . . some filthy kind of animal . . . so I slapped her around a bit . . . guys said she was a funny kind of bim . . . would do it for them standing up, but not for me she wouldn't . . . so I slapped her around . . .

Magistrate nods and makes a notation. The light on the Man dies. Rita Joe speaks with urgency and growing fear to Steve Laporte.

Rita. . . . Then you shut the wipers off an' we just sitting there, not knowing what to do . . . I wish . . . we could go back again there an' start living' from that day on—Jaimie!

Rita looks at Steve as at a stranger, she stands and draws away from him. Jaimie enters behind Rita. Cold light before Magistrate again, and an older man moves into the light, replacing the first witness. He, too, is one of the Murderers. The older man testifies with full gusto.

Older Man. Gave her a job in my tire store . . . took her over to my place after work once . . . she was scared when I tried a trick—but I'm easy on broads that get scared, providin' they keep their voices down . . . After that, I slipped her a fiver . . . well, she took the money, then she stood in front of the window, her head high an' her naked shoulders shakin' like she was cold. Well, sir, she cried a little an' then she says, "Goddamnit, but I wish I was a school teacher . . . " *(laughs and everyone on stage joins in the laugh)*

Light dies out on Older Man. The Indian Boys stand and with the murderers turn their backs to audience like tombstones in a graveyard. Jaimie crosses to Rita and they lie together and make love. Sounds of wind made vocally by the cast.

Rita. You always came to see me, Jaimie Paul . . . the night we were in the cemetery . . . you remember, Jaimie Paul? I turned my face from yours until I saw the ground . . . an' I knew that below us . . . they were like us once, and now they lie below the ground, their eyes gone, the bones showin' . . . they must've spoke and touched each other here . . . Like you're touching me, Jaimie Paul . . . an' now there was nothing over them, except us . . . an' wind in the grass an' a barbwire fence creaking. An' behind that, a hundred acres of barley. *(Jaimie stands.)* That's somethin to remember, when you're lovin', eh?

Sound of a train whistle, Jaimie goes and the lights on stage fade down. Up music and Singer sings. As Jaimie passes her, Singer pursues Jaimie up the ramp, and Rita runs after them.

Singer *(sings).* Oh can't you see that train roll on
Gonna kill a man, before it's gone—
Jaimie Paul fell and died
He had it comin', so it's all right—
Silver train with wheels on fire!

Whiteoaks

Mazo de la Roche

Published 1936
First production London, England, 1936, by Little Theatre

From Act II, Scene 2
Characters in the excerpt: Renny, Finch, Piers, Wakefield

Mazo de la Roche (1885-1961) was born in Toronto. Although of English, Irish and French descent, she was given a Spanish masculine name in memory of one of her father's friends. She was educated at home and began writing at an early age. So that she could illustrate her own books, she decided to study drawing at the University of Toronto, but soon devoted herself entirely to writing. Best known as a novelist, Mazo de la Roche published her first book in 1922, and the Jalna series began to appear in 1927.

In 1972, C.B.C. launched the ambitious but disastrous television drama series of adaptations from the Jalna books, perhaps in an attempt to match the B.B.C.'s internationally successful adaptation of John Galsworthy's *Forsyte Saga*. But in 1936, Mazo de la Roche had already adapted her own *Whiteoaks of Jalna* (1929) for the stage, and it is from this adaptation that our excerpt is taken. It is actually a far livelier piece than any of the C.B.C. episodes, and in its own day, this adaptation was performed in London and New York.

Our excerpt illustrates the author's interest in family conflict and the upsurge of artistic temperament in the Whiteoaks family. The problems of the maturing personality are dramatized in a menacing situation, the crossexamination of a victim. The weight of moral disapproval and the melodramatic feeling which dominate this scene are perhaps further suggested by the massive, old-fashioned and expensive furnishings of the Whiteoaks' living room in which the action takes place one late afternoon.

The curtain rises on the Whiteoaks' living-room, large, old-fashioned, and well-furnished in a rather heavy style; the window curtains drawn. Prominently placed are two oil paintings. One is of an officer in the uniform of a Captain of a British regiment in India of the period 1850. The other is a handsome young auburn-haired woman in low-cut evening dress of the same time. On the sideboard stands a good deal of massive silver.

Renny, with uprolled sleeves, is rubbing Merlin with a large towel. Piers, pipe in mouth, is directing the operation while lounging against the mantelpiece. Wakefield, perched on the edge of the table, is eating a chocolate bar.

Renny. Good boy! Good boy! Soon over! He knows every word I say.

Piers. Rub him well behind the ears! How the hell did he get in such a mess?

Wakefield. He was in the coal cellar after a rat.

Piers. I'll bet you put him up to it. I'll get another towel. *(He goes out.)*

Wakefield. Will you give me fifty cents, Renny?

Renny. No!

(Pause.)

Wakefield. Well, twenty-five cents then.

Renny. Good dog! Good dog! *(pause)*

Wakefield. Please, Renny. Ten cents.

Renny. I gave you ten cents yesterday and you spent it on chocolates.

Wakefield. There's nothing else to do with ten cents! If I had a dollar I would buy something that would be good for me.

Renny. I'll see. *(rising and relighting his pipe)*

Wakefield. What will Aunt Augusta say to Merlin being washed here?

Renny. No more rats for you, my boy.

Wakefield. Finch has plenty of money. It's not fair!

Renny. Finch plenty of money! Hm!

Wakefield. Well, he buys cigarettes, and he goes to theatres and concerts. I've seen programs.

Renny grunts and renews the energetic rubbing. Piers comes in with Finch by the arm. When they are inside he looses him and gives him a push. Finch staggers a little. He is pale and dishevelled and slightly intoxicated.

Piers. I found him in the passage . . . sneaking in the back way, so I brought him along.

Wakefield. He does look funny.

Finch glares at them in stupid resentment.

Finch. What are you staring at?

Piers. I believe you've been drinking.

Renny *(still rubbing Merlin).* Huh! Finch drinking!

Wakefield *(sniffing at Finch).* Whisky, I should think. *(sniffing again)* I'm sure.

Piers. Have you? Have you?

Finch. Well, I felt so rotten. I only had one. I wish I hadn't now.

Piers. Only one?

Renny. Is this true, Finch?

Finch. Yes.

Renny. When?

Finch. About an hour ago.

Renny. Where have you been all the morning?

Finch. I got up late. I felt so rotten.

Renny. Here, Wake—take Merlin and run along.

Wakefield. I'd rather—*(gets down from table)*

Renny. Get out!

Wakefield reluctantly goes out, taking Merlin.

Renny. Now then! What were you doing last night?

Finch. I was in town.

Renny. Yes, I know that. You were supposed to be spending the night with a friend studying, but you weren't, were you?

Finch. No.

Renny. Where were you?

Finch. I—oh—I—can't—

Renny. Don't mumble! Where were you?

Finch *(desperately).* Playing in an orchestra.

Renny. An orchestra!

Piers. What orchestra?

Finch. An orchestra I belong to. I—

Renny. Come now! Come now!

Finch. There is no harm in it.

Renny. What sort of orchestra?

Piers. He's the crooner. I'll bet he's the crooner!

Finch. Oh, just an orchestra that a few fellows got up.

Piers. Oh—h!

Finch. We wanted to make some money.

Piers. And what do you do?

Finch. I play the piano.

Piers. Oh—you play the piano!

Renny. Shut up, Piers. *(to Finch)* Who are the other fellows?

Finch. Some fellows I know—I just got in with them.

Piers. Oh, you just got in with them!

Finch. Yes. We practise after school.

Renny. Where do you play?

Finch. In restaurants. Cheap ones—for dances.

Renny. You persuaded me *(going a bit closer)* to let you spend your nights in town so that you might study with another boy, and this is what you were up to! Who are these fellows? Who *are* they?

Finch. You wouldn't know if I told you.

Renny. Are they students?

Finch. No. But they work. One in a greenhouse. One in some sort of tailoring job.

Piers. How much did you get for playing?

Finch. Five dollars a night.

Renny. And after the dance is over you knock about the town drinking, eh?

Finch *(wringing his fingers together).* No, no, this is the very first time. I was awfully tired. They gave me something to buck me up. Not much. It was pretty rotten stuff, and when we came out into the street we—couldn't find our way at first—it was raining hard—and—and—

Renny turns from him with a gesture of distaste.

Renny. You're in no condition to listen to me now. Go to bed and sleep it off.

Piers. If you were mine, I'd put your head in Merlin's bath and sober you.

Finch *(hoarsely).* But I'm not yours! I'm not anybody's. You talk as though I were a dog!

Piers. I wouldn't insult a dog by comparing him to you!

Finch *(loudly).* And you'll not insult me! I'm not afraid of you!

He advances threateningly towards Piers, who doubles his fists.

Renny. Don't touch him, Piers! He's half drunk!

Finch. I'm not drunk! Come on! Come on!

Finch begins to cough, pulls a soiled handkerchief from his pocket and blows his nose. A crumpled half-sheet of note-paper falls to the floor.

Piers *(picking up the paper and examining it).* What's this? Another lottery ticket; you're quite a gambler.

Finch. Give it to me! It's mine!

Piers pushes him off, smooths out the paper and casts his eyes over it. His face darkens.

Piers. A letter of yours, eh? Listen to this, Renny! "Darling Finch." My God! That this sort of muck should be written to a brother of mine! Here, Renny, read it yourself. Who the hell is this Arthur?

Finch. He's a friend of mine, he helps me with my music.

Renny *(after reading the letter).* I'm disgusted with you!

Finch feels annihilated. His face is drawn.

Finch. I don't understand!

Piers. He doesn't *understand!*

Renny. Do you know what this leads to?

Finch. The orchestra?

Renny. No, not the orchestra! *(striking the letter)* I'd rather you had spent last night in a brothel than to find you carrying that sloppy letter about! *(He tosses the letter into the fireplace.)*

Finch. What's it all about? I don't understand.

Renny. This man is no friend for you, whoever he is!

Finch. But Renny—

Renny. He's a rotter. You'll keep away from him in future. Can you understand that?

Piers. What have you done with the money you've earned by the orchestra?

Finch. I spent it on concerts—to hear music.

Renny. Concerts—my God, more music—to make you more spineless.

Finch *(eagerly).* Music means nothing to you! It is everything to me! My brain is never so clear as when I'm listening to music. Never so clear and free. Arthur knows a lot about music. I like going to concerts with him. What's wrong with that?

Renny. How many piano lessons are left in this term?

Finch. Two.

Renny. There will be no more lessons till you've passed your exams. Neither will you play the piano at home or anywhere else. You are not to put your hands on a keyboard until you pass your exams, do you understand that? *(turning sharply to Piers)* Come on, Piers. We have wasted enough time this afternoon.

Renny goes. Piers picks up the bath.

Piers *(to Finch with a jocular air).* I think we'll tell Gran of this. She'll take it out of you with her stick!

He follows Renny out.

Finch *(shouting).* She's the only one who understands . . . *(Stands motionless for a space, then picks up the letter from where it has fallen and reads it carefully.)* But what is wrong with this letter?

A pause—then his face is illuminated by understanding. He wildly tears the letter into several pieces and throws them into the fire. He stands irresolute, staring at the piano. He picks up the towel from the floor. He winds it about his neck and draws it tight. He sways a little. He is choking himself. Then, horror at what he is doing sweeps over him. He drops the towel. He sinks with a gasp of relief to the piano seat. There is a pause, then he brings his hands down in a wild tumult of sound, challenging and triumphant.

Creeps

David Freeman

Published 1972
First production, Toronto, 1970, by Factory Lab Theatre

Characters in the excerpt: Jim, Tom, Sam, Pete

David Freeman was born in Toronto in 1944. He attended Sunnyview School for the Handicapped until he was 17 years old, when he transferred to a sheltered workshop. In 1966 he enrolled at McMaster University and later graduated with a B.A. in political science.

Creeps is a play written out of Freeman's own experience of disability and the routine of existence in a sheltered workshop. The play takes its title from the slang name given to such cerebral palsy victims as the ones represented by the characters in our excerpt. It is a name by which they also refer to themselves. In doing so they feel, and make us feel, their intense frustration and humiliation. In the play we get an insight into a world of feebleness, frustration and sterility in which the characters exist under the supervision of Carson. Two of the men, Jim and Tom, are trying to make a break with institutional living by deciding to live in the outside world and survive by developing their artistic talents. Only Tom, at the end of the play, has the courage to leave.

First performed at the Factory Lab Theatre, the play was revised for a production at the Tarragon Theatre, Toronto, in October, 1971. The revised text was published in 1972, and it is from this that our excerpt is taken. *Creeps* won the first Chalmers Award for the outstanding Canadian play of 1972 as a result of judging by the Toronto Drama Bench, a newly formed organization of drama critics in the Toronto area.

Our excerpt, taken from near the end of the play, shows Tom attempting to convince Jim to set up an independent life with him in the difficult and dangerous outside world. The acting challenges are difficult, calling for sensitive and compassionate observation of the grotesque gestures of such handicapped people: bodies must be contorted and speech sometimes distorted (though never unclear) to convey the strain and the difficulties of the crippled. The playwright's own helpful notes on the characters' movements are an excellent and moving guide. They are reprinted here before the excerpt itself. The play takes place in the men's washroom of the sheltered workshop.

Some Notes on the Characters' Movements

Each actor taking a role of one of the characters with cerebral palsy is faced, as the character, with major physical problems, the practical solution of which is paramount to a successful rendering of the play. It is to be noted that there are many kinds of spasticity, and each actor should base his movements on one of these. There can be no substitute for the first-hand observation of these physical problems, and one might even suggest that the play not be attempted if opportunities for such first-hand observation are not available. These notes indicate the approach taken by the actors in the original production.

Pete
The actor in the original production developed a way of speaking that is common to many spastics. The effort required to speak causes a distortion of the facial muscles. The actor was able to achieve this by thrusting the jaw forward, and letting the lower jaw hang. Whatever speech problem is adopted for this role, no actor should attempt it unless he has an opportunity for first hand observation.

The deformed hand was not held rigid in one position. The actor used the hand for many things, keeping the fist clenched and employing the fingers in a clawlike manner.

Jim
The actor walked with his knees almost touching, feet apart, back bent much of the time, using his arms more than any other part of his body for balance.

Sam
Sam is a diaplegic, his body dead from the waist down (except for his genitals). He is in a wheelchair. The problem for this actor was to find how to make the wheelchair an extension of his body.

A men's washroom in a sheltered workshop. The hall leading to the washroom is visible. In the washroom are two urinals and two stalls. A chair is set against one of the stalls and there is a bench.

Jim. Tom, what is it?

Tom. I'm quitting.

Jim. You're not serious?

Tom. Getting more serious by the minute.

Jim. You're building a lot on a few kind words, aren't you?

Tom. The man doesn't know I'm spastic.

Jim. He's going to find out. And you know what'll happen when he does. You'll be his golden boy for a few weeks, but as soon as the novelty wears off, he'll go out of his way to avoid you.

Tom. What if the novelty doesn't wear off?

Jim. Tom, I don't think you should rush into this.

Tom. How long do I have to stay, Jim?

Jim. Stay until Christmas. Stay and do the mural.

Tom. No.

Jim. But you like painting. It won't hurt you.

Tom. I said no!

Jim. Why not?

Tom moves towards the door.

Jim. Won't you at least talk about it?

Tom *(He turns and looks at Jim).* That's all you know how to do now, isn't it? No writing, no thinking, just talking. Well get this straight. I don't want any part of the Spastic Club or the Workshop. It's finished, okay?

Jim. Look, I know this place isn't perfect. I agree. It's even pretty rotten at times. But, Tom, out there, you'll be lost. You're not wanted out there, you're not welcome. None of us are. If you stay here we can work together. We can build something.

Sam. Yeah, a monument to Carson. For the pigeons to shit on.

Tom. How long are *you* going to stay here?

Jim. How long?

Tom. Are you going to spend the rest of your life being Carson's private secretary?

Jim. Well, nothing's permanent. Even I know that.

Jim. Stop bullshitting and give me a straight answer.

Jim. Okay, I'll move on. Sure.

Tom. And do what?

Jim. Maybe I'll go back to my writing.

Tom When? *(no reply)* When was the last time you wrote anything?

Jim. Last month I wrote an article for "The Sunshine Friend."

Pete *(joined by Sam).* "You are my sunshine, my only sunshine . . . "

Tom. Shut up! I mean when was the last time you wrote something you wanted to write?

Jim. Well, you know, my typewriter's bust . . .

Tom. Don't give me that crap about your typewriter. You don't want to get it fixed.

Jim. That's not true . . .

Tom. Do you know what you're doing here? You're throwing away your talent for a lousy bit of security.

Jim. Tom, you don't understand . . .

Tom. You're wasting your time doing a patch up job at something you don't really believe in. *(Jim does not reply, Tom moves towards him.)* Jim, there are stacks of guys in this world who haven't the intelligence to know where they're at. But you have. You *know*. And if you don't *do* something with that knowledge, you'll end up hating yourself.

Jim. What the hell could I do?

Tom. You could go into journalism, write a book. Listen, in this job, who can you tell it to? Spastics. Now think. Think of all the millions of jerks on the outside who have no idea of what it's really like in here. Hell, you could write a best-seller.

Jim. I've thought about it.

Tom. Well *do* something about it.

Jim. Don't you think I want to?

Tom. Jim, I know you're scared. I'm scared. But if I don't take this chance, I won't have a hope in hell of making it. And if you keep on doing something you don't want to do, soon you won't even have a mind. Do you think if Michael had a mind like yours he'd be content to hang around here all day flushing toilets?

Pete. He's right, Jim. You don't belong here. Why don't you and Tom go together?

Tom. Look, I'll help you. We can go, we can get a place, we can do it together. Come on, what do you say?

Branch Plant

Harvey Markowitz

Published 1972
First production Toronto, 1971, by Factory Lab Theatre

Act II, Scene 6
Characters in the excerpt: Blaseley, Vanderhoef, Currie, intercom. voice of Pamela Williams

Harvey Markowitz was born in Toronto in 1933. In 1967 he won a Canada Council Centennial Award, following this up with the award for the best new play in the Central Ontario Drama League competition in 1968. He is a producer of stage plays, and became writer in residence at the St. Lawrence Centre, Toronto, in 1972.

Branch Plant was first put on the stage at Factory Lab Theatre in Toronto in May, 1971. The main situation of the play is the close-down of a Canadian branch factory which belongs to a huge international corporation controlled from London. At the discretion of the director of the play, London could just as well be changed to New York. The situation provides the opportunity for a dramatization of the power structure and impersonal, ruthless methods of big business. The political implications of such a closure are explored through the effects on the union of workers, the feelings of Canadian Nationalism aroused by the possibility that the Canadian managers might be able to keep the plant going under local ownership, and the personal conflicts which arise as men jockey for promotion in the corporation at the expense of friendships, loyalty to the local community and, by extension, to their own country.

Vanderhoef, Canadian manager of the plant, is brought to the point where he sees that as a Canadian he has the opportunity to save the plant from closure and thus save the employees' jobs. He can either make a bid to buy the factory in association with Currie, his chief sales manager, and another colleague, or he can push for government ownership of the factory. We see him, however, submit to both temptation and pressure from his superior, Blaseley, a cunning and unscrupulous man from London. Vanderhoef climbs another rung on the ambition ladder.

Our excerpt reveals that Vanderhoef's choice brings his income up to $50,000 per year, but involves him in the unpleasant task of relieving perfectly competent and hard-working friends and colleagues of their jobs. He has already realized that he might well be working against the best interests of his country by not helping to engineer a Canadian take-over. The setting is the top executive office in the factory.

A large corporate office on the top (fourth) floor of the 'east' building. There is a large window (centre rear) which overlooks the 'west' building and yards.

In the office are a large executive desk and leather chair, four to six stacking chairs. Filing cabinets, book shelves, portraits, symbols, advertising posters and graphs on the walls. In particular they include a portrait of the president of Duntop (England) Limited, a portrait of president of Duntop (Canada) Limited, a photo of Vanderhoef's wife and two children, the degrees and diplomas of Tim Vanderhoef: Degree of Chartered accountant, degree of bachelor of commerce, degree of master of business administration. There is a coffee set and serving table.

Of importance are the two doors for they help the flow of the play immensely. One can be called the exterior door and the other the interior door. The former admits people on business the latter admitting fellow executives and superiors.

A Monday morning, 9:30 A.M. Vanderhoef is at his desk auditing some financial statements when Blaseley knocks and enters.

Blaseley *(putting transfer sheets before him).* Sorry to barge in Tim—the transfers have finally come.

Vanderhoef. Just in time too, rumours were getting wild. *(as he is nervously looking down list)*

Blaseley *(hiding his enjoyment).* No, you're not down there—that's for the rest. A personal message Tim, you're being transferred to Ajax at $50,000.00 per.

Vanderhoef *(relieved).* Yeah, great!

Blaseley. H.O. and Oakcroft like your work and my recommendation did the trick.

Vanderhoef. Good—thanks Alex.

Blaseley. In fact we're both going there.

Vanderhoef *(hides his lack of enthusiasm).* Good, good. *(refuses to dwell on that)* It's a move up.

Blaseley. Certainly is.

Vanderhoef. Lorraine'll be glad to hear. Save a moving trip, she hates moving, so do the kids. What's the assignment?

Blaseley *(as if he would tell him).* Don't know yet. Oakcroft wants to outline it personally. He's set up morning meetings for next week—okay with you?

Vanderhoef *(nodding as he sees diary is clear).* Fine. *(as he writes in)* I'll be there.

Blaseley. I suggest you call a meeting of your Department Heads as soon as possible.

Vanderhoef. Right. Get the speculating over. *(as he returns to reading transfer list)*

Blaseley *(nearing door).* Be up at Ajax if you need me.

Vanderhoef *(has seen the inevitable).* Alex, wait a minute, Currie, Currie's not on here.

Blaseley. Just him 'n Gauthier, the rest are transferred.

Vanderhoef *(extremely agitated).* Look, can you spare a minute.

Blaseley. Certainly. *(coming back, sitting down)*

Vanderhoef. Something must be done, you can't—

Blaseley. Can't?

Vanderhoef *(sputtering).* Why Gauthier?

Blaseley. He didn't cover for me, made me look assinine. *(said mean, cruel)*

Vanderhoef. But in a way it's our fault—

Blaseley. No matter how much experience you learn from every closing: From this one—to hire outside public relations men.

Vanderhoef *(sensing the finality and dismissal in Blaseley's voice).* But Currie?

Blaseley *(a trifle impatient).* That's the list—Head Office approval, triple signed.

Vanderhoef. You said I'd be consulted.

Blaseley. But it was so obvious.

Vanderhoef. They've got to reconsider: twenty years seniority. Let him come with me.

Blaseley. Don't put it up to me, there's Oakcroft and Head Office—I can only make recommendations.

Vanderhoef. What did you recommend?

Blaseley. If you must know I recommended dismissal.

Vanderhoef. Because he wanted to bid for the plant?

Blaseley. No, nothing of the kind. In my judgement he's an old exec. I told you I wouldn't transfer deadwood. It's part of my job, to clear it out.

Vanderhoef. I want to speak to Oakcroft.

Blaseley. Your privilege; if you want to go over my head there's no way I can stop you.

Vanderhoef *(backing down: a forced smile).* I don't want to go over your head. Hell, we've been getting along good. It's just that I've worked with him—he's able, he's not particular. He'll take anything you give him.

Blaseley. Tim there are young men coming up in every branch.

Vanderhoef. Would you mind if I speak to Oakcroft.

Blaseley *(there are many ways to skin the same cat).* No, I don't mind. Maybe it'll help.

Vanderhoef. And would you put in a good word in case you're asked?

Blaseley. Well I can't go too far but if you can find a way for Currie—it's alright with me.

Vanderhoef. So I won't say anything to him.

Blaseley. Why not say it's conditional or . . . contingent—something like that . . . Because he does deserve some notice in case you and Oakcroft . . . *(shrugs)*

Vanderhoef *(seeing the futility).* Yeah. I better tell him something. *(looks at list)* Alex there's more here than you said—why are all these stenos and accounting clerks being chopped?

Blaseley *(impatient).* Just tell the respective department head *(with relish)* Or if you want I'll tell them. I haven't much to do now. *(reaches for list)*

Vanderhoef *(not liking what he sees in Blaseley).* I'll do it.

Blaseley. If you like I can mention to Currie it's contingent.

Vanderhoef. No it's my job.

Blaseley. Think of the bright side: how many are being transferred. *(leaving)* Oakcroft will be wanting a report from me, I'll phone you in an hour. *(exits)*

Vanderhoef, after a moment's hesitation presses intercom.

Williams *(through intercom).* Yes.

Vanderhoef *(to intercom).* Pamela, page Currie and Gauthier. Send them in one at a time.

Williams *(through intercom).* Yes sir.

Vanderhoef walks about for 5 seconds. There is a knock on the door.

Vanderhoef. Come in.

Currie *(entering).* Hello Tim.

Vanderhoef *(as Currie sits).* It's the transfers Dick—they're out. *(hands him the list)* What's there to say. I'm sorry.

Curie *(bravado).* I was prepared for it.

Vanderhoef *(quickly).* But this isn't the end of it—no sir. I'm going to appeal straight to Oakcroft.

It's very important for Currie to do a marvellous bit of acting with this 'bravado' bit. What is necessary is for Currie to hide his true feelings of fear and despair for his future with an over-confidence which doesn't ring true to the audience, i.e. his bravura betrays him.

Currie *(bravura).* Naw don't bother.

Vanderhoef. You don't mean that.

Currie *(bravura)*. Sure I do; I got contacts—I'll be alright.

Vanderhoef. Look have you got enough money?

Currie *(bravura)*. I'm alright.

Vanderhoef. Honest?

Currie *(bravura chuckle)*. Honest.

Vanderhoef. Well I'm going to talk you up.

Currie *(bravura)*. Oh there's lotsa ads in the Engineering bulletin.

Vanderhoef. No I'm going to talk to Oakcroft. Got Blaseley's co-operation.

Currie. Whatever you think best.

Vanderhoef *(pain)*. I tried, honest Dick, I really tried.

Currie. I believe you. It's okay, I know business.

Vanderhoef. Dick, you're fooling me, I know better. Now you're not going to lose your way. Promise me you're not?

Currie *(nods)*. Do me a favour, don't let the word out.

Vanderhoef. What word? You're staying on I told you! *(taking back official notice)*.

Currie. Look this doesn't mean I leave now, I'd like to finish what I'm doing but I don't want the others to know.

Vanderhoef. No one's going to know. You finish that job.

Currie. Thanks. Is that all? *(getting up)*.

Vanderhoef *(nods)*. Let's have lunch soon.

Currie. Sure, sure. *(leaving)*.

Vanderhoef. I'll call you.

Currie. Right.

Exits. Pause. Intercom buzz.

Vanderhoef *(pressing)*. Yes?

Williams *(through intercom)*. Mr. Gauthier. *(Vanderhoef is unable to carry on.)*

Vanderhoef *(to intercom)*. Er . . . ask him to wait a minute will ya.

Williams *(through intercom)*. Yes Mr. Vanderhoef. *Fade Out on Vanderhoef.*

Crabdance

Beverley Simons

Published 1969
First production, Seattle, 1969

From Act II
Characters in the excerpt: Sadie, Highrise, Dickens, Mowchuk

Beverley Simons lives in West Vancouver. She has written poetry, short stories, a novella, scripts for television and film, as well as stage plays. *Crabdance* was first performed in Seattle under the direction of Malcolm Black in 1969, and has recently been performed at the Playhouse Vancouver.

Sadie Golden is not only the play's heroine, but also the structural backbone of its episodic action and the embodiment of its theme. She is bighearted, gregarious, impulsive, and if given the chance, flamboyant; because of the impersonal conditions of modern life, she is forced to be lonely and frustrated. She compensates for her dwindling life by inventing neurotic rituals and maintaining pseudo-relationships with salesmen. These wandering denizens of the modern commercial desert (to her a sea, perhaps) serve as partners in her rituals, figuring in her mind as grand, perhaps extravagant, personages.

The play takes its title from the ritual dance Sadie performs. This dance resembles the mating dance of giant Alaska crabs, and symbolizes Sadie's emotional dependence on the salesmen. The dramatic style of *Crabdance* owes much to that species of intellectual farce which has been called "theatre of the absurd". Sometimes funny, at times grim, it works through a variety of conventions—those of realism, expressionism, symbolism and the music-hall.

Our excerpt, played like a vaudeville skit, exploits the fact that we are watching actors in a play pretending to be people who decide to act like music-hall artistes. Pace and timing are crucial, and the right note of vulgarity and extravagance, as Highrise is applauded for his financial frauds, must be achieved to put across the satire of our society. The setting is Sadie's living room.

Livingroom, diningroom, entrance hall, kitchen, in what appears to be a two story middleclass house. The second story does not exist visually. Freestanding stairs end abruptly in space above the set. The upper portion of the stairs may be obscured at first by a wall or scrim which moves during the glare at the end of the play. Stage front represents a large plate glass window.

The set should be suggestive rather than detailed, and though the furniture as described is real, the effect should be curiously disturbing. The furniture is shrouded in cowl-like sheets. The only piece revealed at the opening is an oldfashioned dining table covered with dusty porcelain teacups and plates. Scattered beside the plates are mounds of writing paper, envelopes, letters, lists. A wall phone hangs between the dining room and kitchen. Pinned beside it is an exaggeratedly long sheet of foolscap covered with names.

A large blue glass cat stands in a conspicuous position on the floor. Scissors, bottles of glue, an open newspaper partly cut, and a scrapbook rest on one of several boxes filled to bursting with advertisements and newspaper clippings.

The smell of mildew mixes with that of freshly baked cakes, pies, tarts, furniture, etc . . . all this before the houselights dim. There must be a rhythm in this play of phone calls, door bells, the buzz or twang of the stove timer, the postman's dumping of the mail, entrances of the "visitors", and, of course, the tug of war rhythm of power between Sadie and her guest "performers."

Sadie is in her 50s, tall, thin, sagging, with graystreaked black hair. She's highly nervous. Smiles appear and disappear involuntarily. She makes little noises without being aware of them. She emanates a strange combination of vulnerability and threat, naivete and cunning. Sounds of Sadie grunting even as the audience settles. She mumbles to herself and her cat, puts in pulls out baking, writes notes, letters, checks her cash, licks envelopes, takes out teacups, dusts them, adjusts bread.

There must be an element of farce in the production.
Faces, costume, set, and action hint at the grotesque.

The following sequence is played like a vaudeville skit.

Highrise. I'm working as a car salesman in a clip joint, see. And when I say clip joint, I'm not just kidding. The owner not only takes the wool from the sheep, he takes the skin. This guy is so crooked he has to have a special bed made like a pretzel to fit him. So I decide, as I have a strong sense of justice, my downfall, ladies and gentlemen, to get one back at the owner on behalf of all the little folk. I sacrifice myself for them, as I do every day of my life.

Dickens *(sarcastically to Mowchuk).* Have you got a hanky?

Highrise. Besides, he's handed me a few soft checks.

Sadie *(prompting).* You take a car.

Highrise. Not just a car. *(He pulls off another sheet off old tea trolley.)* A Jaguar XKE.

Mowchuk. Is that better than a Lincoln?

Highrise. So long, suckers! I've taken your debts on me, your dreams, and your hate. Blessed and cleansed be your pocketbooks! They read the papers and, man, they wish me luck like I'm an athlete, every one of 'em wanting to be me but knowing he doesn't have the guts. The lights of the small towns come and go. Come and go. *(appropriate light effects by Sadie)* Young girls turn over in their beds and moan as I pass. Then dawn. *(He stops. Sadie uncovers a sign: Wetaskiwin. Highrise shrugs.)* Why not? It's as good as Chicoutemi. I enter their lives like a comet. *(He approaches Dickens.)* Excuse me, is this Wetaskiwin?

Dickens. What?

Sadie. Answer him. Go on. Say, "Yes, it is, Mr. Looking for anything in particular?" Say it. You're an old cleaning man in the train station.

Highrise. Torn overalls, yellow moustache, pushing a broom . . .

Sadie. The smell of banana and orange peel, gum wrappers, half-eaten wieners . . .

Dickens. Have you gone mad?

Sadie. Are you going to play, or would you like to leave?

Dickens *(grudgingly playing role).* Are you looking for anyone in particular?

Highrise. Why, yes, my good man . . . *(Dickens bristles).*

Sadie *(warning).* Mr. Dickens . . . He can keep his name, can't he, Highrise?

Dickens. No-one in my family has been in sanitation.

Highrise *(in play).* As a matter of fact, I'm looking for the mayor.

Dickens. How would you expect a janitor to know the mayor?

Sadie. You have that part, too.

Dickens. A mayor, eh? That's more like it. What was he like? A man of dignity, I'd imagine, with the proper word for . . .

Highrise. With a paunch and a silver pocket watch and a passingly pretty daughter of about . . . eighteen. *(Sadie strikes a pose.)* Delightful.

Dickens *(in role).* May I be of help to you, sir?

Highrise. I'm looking for a printer to make . . . *(takes out colorful lease form perhaps large size).*

Sadie. Copies of a copy of a leasing form.

Dickens. I'd be glad to oblige, but why ask me such a thing?

Highrise. Well, you see, I, or rather my company, have reason to suspect that the land around your little town, your charming town of Wetaskiwin . . . *(Looks around as though to check if anyone is listening.)* Mr. Mayor, would you like to become the official most likely to be remembered in the entire history of this region? Instead of being the mayor of Wetaskiwin, the trade center of the grain belt, how would you like to be mayor of Wetaskiwin, Oil Center of the North?

Dickens. Oil?

Mowchuk. Oil.

Sadie. Copies of a copy of a . . . *(Highrise, from his magical pockets, produces shares and agreements for Dickens and Mowchuk to sign.)* Go on. Sign.

Mowchuk. I don't sign anything I haven't read.

Dickens. A man's reputation rests in his name.

Sadie. An investment, too.

Dickens. Money?

Sadie. He'll give it back after. Won't you?

Highrise. Scout's honor.

Mowchuk. This is a contract for a share in a brick company.

Sadie. Highrise, don't be naughty. *(Highrise takes back and exchanges papers for others.)* Money, gentlemen. *(They give some grudgingly. Highrise tips his hat, and, facing an imaginary congregation, clears his throat).*

Highrise. I am indeed privileged to be addressing this distinguished assembly of the town council, as well as interested fellow citizens, who have kindly gathered here tonight. I assure you that this honor will be repaid in the same spirit in which it is given.

Sadie. Hip hip . . .

All. Hooray!

Highrise. I have with me news that the first drilling begins . . . in a couple of weeks.

Sadie. Hip, hip . . .

Highrise. Men and machinery are now on their way to Wetaskiwin . . .

All. Hooray!

Highrise. There will be full employment.

Sadie. Hip, hip . . .

Highrise. And all for the smallest contribution on your part.

Silence. Highrise sits ceremoniously, hand out, waiting for the money. Neither of the men budge.

He Didn't Even Say Goodbye

Norman Williams

Published 1972
Televised 1966, by C.B.C.

Characters in the excerpt: Ben, Saunders, Dr. Bagler, Alice

    Born in Toronto in 1923, Norman Williams has written many radio and stage plays over the last twenty years. In 1953 he took first prize in the Ottawa Little Theatre One-Act Competition. Some of his plays, such as *A Battle of Wits* (1953) and *Protest* (1956), have an oriental appeal, while others create fantasy in an historical setting and with period costuming. His collection *Worlds Apart* (1956) contains several of his short plays.

    He Didn't Even Say Goodbye, adapted for television and broadcast on CBC Television in 1966, uses a contemporary setting, a suburban house, in which to explore the world of Ben, a business executive, who suffers from a curious syndrome: Ben's brain has developed the habit of refusing to perceive in any way at all the presence of persons who irritate or anger him. The result is that they simply fade out of Ben's apprehension and disappear. When this affliction attacks him in the midst of his own family, Ben misses work and keeps to his room. Ben realises that he must try to control his negative feelings toward people, and learn to love again. It is interesting to compare this situation with Kafka's horrifying treatment of the same theme of alienation from human life in his story *Metamorphosis*. Ben's efforts are bound to fail, for his wife, Alice, has made food a substitute for love, while his son has learned never to display his emotions but concentrate with icy determination on the study of law.

    In our scene, set in Ben's room at home, Williams neatly uses Ben's ailment for light comic purposes to satirize the bright and breezy manner and obtuseness of Dr. Bagler. Ben's only real contact is with his colleague, Saunders, a friend from the office.

Enter Dr. Bagler, a crisp man, followed by Alice.

Ben. Not you, too, Alice.

Saunders. I think she should stay, Ben.

Bagler *(to Ben).* Well, well, and how are we today?

Ben. Well enough to be let alone.

Bagler. That's not what I've been hearing. *(winks at Saunders)* Any pain? Now, don't hold anything back. Pain is nature's warning signal. Like a train whistle at a crossing. We pay heed to those, don't we?

Ben *(to Saunders)*. It's happening.

Bagler. Where? Where do you feel pain?

Ben *(to Saunders)*. Gone.

Bagler. Gone? Well, where was it? Let me see your tongue.

Ben *(to Saunders)*. I told you he would.

Bagler. I'm trying to help you. *(angrily)* But if you're going to refuse to co-operate with me . . .

Ben. It was inevitable.

Bagler *(going to Alice)*. Inevitable? What does he mean inevitable? *(comes back to Ben)* Refusing to co-operate may be inevitable to your mind.

Ben. Why don't you say something?

Bagler. I am saying something. I am speaking to you, sir.

Saunders. Perhaps if he rested now and you came back tonight, Doctor . . .

Bagler. We can't let hours go by. This may be serious. *(to Ben)* And if you're wise, you'll adopt a serious attitude towards it.

Ben. Is he still here?

Saunders. Doctor, in his present state of mind . . .

Bagler. In *his* state of mind, he should be in hospital.

Ben. Why don't you go, Alice?

Bagler. Why should your wife go to hospital? You're the one . . .

Ben *(to Saunders)*. She annoys me standing there fidgeting . . . ravenous to attack my left-overs.

Bagler. Is that any reason to put her in the hospital? The man is not rational.

Ben. He'll want to put me in the hospital next. That's his solution to everything that puzzles him. Passing the buck is what it amounts to.

Bagler *(fuming)*. Now, sir, you may be ill, but you're just as perverse and insulting as you are ill. Never in my professional career have I passed the buck to anybody. And I demand an apology from you for saying I have.

Ben. Why doesn't somebody say something?

Bagler. Oh, the man is impossible! *(He shoves everything into his bag and slaps it shut.)*

Ben. Is he gone?

Bagler. No, but he's going.

Alice. Doctor, I really don't believe he's himself. Do you?

Ben *(pleased).* Ah, there he goes.

Exit doctor followed by Alice.

Saunders *(concerned).* I doubt if you'll see him again.

Ben. Literally.

Saunders. He might have helped you.

Ben. That false jollity. 'Well, well, and how are we today?'

Party Day

Jack Winter

Published 1972. First production in Ottawa, June 1969, Studio Theatre, National Arts Centre.

Characters in the excerpt as in the original script: Joseph Goebbels (also plays Mulqueen, voices of Lewald, Barrington-Hudson, Baillet-Latour, Sherrill), Leni Riefenstahl (also plays W.A.S.P., voice of Austria), Albert Speer (also plays Minister, voices of Attila, Capek, Brecht), Hans Fritzsche (also plays voice of Fritzsche)

Alternative arrangement of characters: Fritzsche, Lewald, Attila, Barrington-Hudson, Baillet-Latour, Sherrill, Goebbels, Speer, Mulqueen, Minister, Kapek, and Riefenstahl, W.A.S.P., Austria.

Jack Winter was born at Moose Jaw, Saskatchewan in 1936. He took his B.A. and M.A. in English at McGill University, and has twice won a Canada Council award. He has been active as a journalist, was resident playwright for Toronto Workshop Productions from 1963-67, and is now a writer for films and theatre.

Party Day was commissioned by the National Arts Centre in Ottawa for the opening of the Studio Theatre there in June, 1969. The play takes a satirical look at state subsidy of the arts, and at international hypocrisy, by focussing our attention on a Goebbels spectacular, the Nurnberg Party Day of the Nazis in 1934, and the Berlin Olympics of 1936. A multi-level stage and a multi-media format provide interesting possibilities for the use of pre-recorded voices, projections, music and graphics. Selected events in Europe prior to World War II provide the situation and plot; historical and representative figures provide the characters; and the persecution of Jews and the appropriation of neighbouring countries by the Nazis provide a grim counterpoint to the running commentary which reveals the organization, ideals, hypocrisy and propaganda connected with the Third Reich. Hitler's state is seen as some enormous and diabolic form of theatrical art created by those warped masters of mass psychology and pageantry, Goebbels and Speer. The whole question of state involvement in physical and artistic culture is thus brought into the particular arena of the stage.

Because the staging conditions are so important to the play, they are given here together with the excerpt. The opportunities are exciting and the challenges here are varied. Tone is of the utmost importance in the delivery of the long monologues; variety and contrast must be stressed to avoid the danger of monotonous similarity in the voices. In the original production, the entire play was performed by only four characters, Fritzsche, Goebbels, Speer and Riefenstahl. Their voices had been pre-recorded in the other parts to be used on the wands and the loud speakers. The excerpt given may be performed in this way or may be staged for twelve characters according to the size of the group and the recording equipment available.

Production Notes

PARTY DAY was first presented in the Studio Theatre of the National Arts Centre (Ottawa, Canada). The following notes refer to that theatre and to that presentation.

The Studio Theatre *is a large three-storey-high room the most important features of which are: a removable ceiling grid; a flat floor, one large section of which is an hydraulic elevator with traps; two narrow galleries which surround the room at the level of the second and the third storeys. The seats are individual and fixed on a series of bleacher-type risers; each chair is free to swivel.*

The house *was enclosed by two-storey-high white drapes hung banner-like and stationary along the walls. The seats were arranged so that there were several acting areas among the audience, as well as a wide central aisle leading to the largest acting area which contained the elevator and trap. Several drapes flew down at times so as to frame the centre aisle and complete the total enclosure of each half of the house. The largest acting area was backed by two staircases leading up to four acting areas on the second level: one at the head of each staircase, one at the front of the house, one at the rear. The musician's gallery was on the third level at the front.*

The visuals *were projected onto the various drapes. They were slide projections operated from a battery of projectors of three different types. Movie projection was used only once (near the end of the play).*

The music *was composed for the "Moog synthesizer" (an electronic keyboard instrument) and was played live by one performer.*

The sound *included taped transmissions and live transmissions (the four acting areas on the second level had standing mikes), and was transmitted over many speakers. Some of the tape was transmitted over "wands": small hand-held transistorized radio receivers (generally used at conferences for simultaneous translations, in museums for "radio-tours", etc.). Each member of the audience was equipped with a "wand". A distinctive call-sound broadcast over the "wands" preceeded each wand-transmission.*

Although visuals *and* music *accompanied the whole of the play, no attempt has been made to describe them in the production notes included with this text.*

> In Party Day many of the speeches are intended to be spoken simultaneously. Therefore, they have been placed on facing pages. For this play all facing pages should be read together, as if they were parallel columns.

Voices of Fritzsche and Lewald on speakers.

Fritzsche. Dr. Theodor Lewald, chairman of the German Olympic Committee.

Lewald. Regarding the ineligibility of Miss Greta Bergman, the high-jumping champion of Wurtenberg: may I point out that only members of the Wurtenberg Light Athletic Association are allowed to compete for positions on the German National Olympic Team, and the Wurtenberg Light Athletic Association does not permit membership to Jews. As chairman of the German Olympic Committee, I consider this matter to be the exclusive concern of the Wurtenberg Light Athletic Association, and absolutely no violation of our avowed international policy of equal opportunity. In any case, Miss Bergman is only the second-best lady high-jumper in Germany, even if she is the best lady high-jumper in Wurtenberg. Regarding the denial to Jews in Germany of the use of all athletic fields, stadia, gymnasia, courts and swimming pools—regarding the exclusion of Jews in Germany from membership in all associations that sponsor sports events and in all youth, welfare and gymnastic societies—regarding the ban on all athletic competition among Jews in Germany and between Jews in Germany and non-Jews in Germany or elsewhere: may I point out that recognized German athletes belong to the German League for Physical Exercise and the qualification for the German League for Physical Exercise is ideological fitness. Besides, clubs have the right to choose their members, don't they? Does the New York Athletic Club have Jewish members? I can tell you that it does not.

Fritzsche and Barrington-Hudson on speakers.

Fritzsche. Desmond Barrington-Hudson, sports commentator for the British Broadcasting Corporation.

Barrington-Hudson. May I say that it is my impression that the splendid organization of Sport in Germany has not made the Germans any less sportsmanlike than they were before they had a Ministry of Sport. Moreover, His Majesty's Government views the coming Olympics as a valuable assurance of European peace. This belief is based on the high importance Germany places upon the Games, and the correspondingly high probability that Germany will make no political or other moves which might force the curtailment or the cancellation of the Olympic programme. This is the foundation of the belief of His Majesty's Government that there is no immediate danger of German reoccupation of the Rhineland. As for the lamentable incident in which a German-Jew football player was kicked to death, may I point out that the game was not an Olympic qualification match.

Voices of Fritzsche and Baillet-Latour on speakers.

Fritzsche. Count Baillet-Latour, President of the International Olympic Committee.

Baillet-Latour. We have had an interview with Dr. Lewald and he has convinced us that Germany will provide a cordial reception to all athletes regardless of race, religion, or political persuasion. And Dr. Lewald agrees that the campaign in support of an anti-Olympic games in Barcelona, Spain is the work of men who do not understand the significance of international sport. It was French soldiers who found and restored the temple of Zeus. It was German soldiers who uncovered the complete site of the ancient games. It is Greece that has retained and glorified every piece of Olympic marble. Olympia! There is a symbol superior to national, religious, military matters. Oarsmen, runners, fencers! there is the free

Voice of Attila on wand.

Attila. Hey bourgeois! Hey proletarian! I, Attila Jozsef, poet, I am here! I, Attila Jozsef, in this contorted Budapest. Fly, poem! Speak out, poem! We are still alive! There is still hope. There is still time if we grab it by the ear. Fly, poem, speak out poem! Call the persevering poor! Chew into them! Tell them it is not imperative to be a hero. God, the Lord, is long. The bacon is short. The poor are as miserable as if they were the rich. God is long and hard and owned by bishops. The poor need Him, too, to increase business. Nothing's poorer than a man who's poor. His shivering he lends to winter; his empty moods to the empty fields. Nothing, nothing, nothing's poorer than a man who's poor.

Hey bourgeois! Hey proletarian! I Attila Jozsef, poet, I am here! I, Attila Jozsef, in this contorted Budapest. My mother died and now I do not know how to behave with her. She would patch my coat; she would look at how beautiful I was naked. The peasants have returned from the harvest; now they are waiting on little benches for death. We want better dinners because we want to be better. We want more pairs of shoes because we want to be more. But my mother slowly merges with the fog and there are bayonets on the opposity shore. Hey! bourgeois! Hey proletarian! I, Attila Jozsef, poet, I am here! I, Attila Jozsef, in this contorted Budapest, I sit on the lowest step of the dock. I watch the melon rinds float by. As if it had its source in me, the Danube is great, wise, confused. They can note what I say on the telephone: when, why, and to whom. They can collect my dreams in dossiers, those who understand them. And I can never guess when they will think there is sufficient reason to pull out that one file that will kill me.

Oh, this is not how I imagined order! This is not my soul's kind of country. I do not believe in a life where it is easier to live if one is underhanded. I do not believe in a people that is frightened at elections and cheerful to bury. Hey, bourgeois! Hey proletarian! I, Attila Jozsef, poet, I am here! I, Attila Jozsef, in this contorted Budapest. Come freedom! You gave birth to him. Now teach him with kind words and let him play sometimes: I, Attila Jozsef, your beautiful, serious son.

trade of the future. The Olympic Games! there is the spirit of Beethoven's Ninth Symphony. Let all men know: we possess the power to remove the games from Berlin even today, and would do so if we felt the Olympic statutes were not being observed in every way. But we see no reason to be influenced by agitation originating from a political source. The sporting world stands behind us: and for this reason in nineteen thirty-six the only legitimate Olympiad will be held in Berlin.

Fritzsche on mike at the radio-desk.

Fritzsche. July twenty-eight, nineteen hundred and thirty-six, Budapest, Hungary. This is Hans Fritzsche. The Olympic torch passed through the Hungarian capital this morning. President Gyula Gombos, loyal ally of the Reich in all matters, explained that the strangely deserted streets were due to the sadness of the Hungarian people at the news of the death of Dr. Theodor Lewald, Chairman of the German Olympic Committee, who committed suicide yesterday because of the discovery of his Jewish origins. Because of Dr. Lewald's administrative contribution, the main street in Berlin Olympic Village will be named after his profession.

Voices of Fritzsche and Sherrill on speakers.

Fritzsche. General Charles H. Sherrill, United States representative on the International Olympic Committee.

Sherrill. Olympic rules govern the selection, not the training of athletes. I do not agree that Germany's withholding of training facilities from Jews violates the Olympic code. Even if such matters were the concern of American athletes, I know what their opinion is. My organization sent a questionnaire to all American athletes who hold Olympic records. Of the hundred and thirty-nine replies, only one opposed participation. Speaking as an American, I see a grave danger in this Olympic controversy. If United States athletes see their own legitimate ambitions frustrated by the few Jews among them, we are certain to have a wave of anti-semitism among those qualified boys and girls who never before gave it a thought. Now they will think that about five million Jews in this country are using white athletes representing one hundred and twenty million Americans to work out something to help the German Jews.

Goebbels, Speer, Riefenstahl enter on the first level and move up the stairs to the front of the second level where they sit. They are transparently disguised (eye-glasses, beads, etc.) as Mulqueen, Minister, W.A.S.P. respectively.

Sherrill *(cont'd).*
And may I take this opportunity to express my respect for Benito Mussolini, a man whom I have long admired, a brave father who sent his own two sons into the thick of fighting, a gallant warrior whom I earnestly wish had the opportunity to come to these United States and suppress Communism here as he has done in Italy.

Fritzsche on mike at the radio-desk.

Fritzsche. July twenty-ninth nineteen hundred and thirty-six Vienna Austria. This is Hans Fritzsche. This evening one hundred thousand Austrians cheered as the Olympic torch was carried once around the Ringstrasse on its way through Vienna. "Holy flame, take our greetings to Berlin!" they chanted in perfect, though spontaneous, synchronization. Reports of bloody riots generated by Na-

Voice of Austria on wand.

Austria. They shot the socialists at half-past five in the name of a victorious Austria in the laughing city of wine and waltzes and starving children, the great ghost: Vienna. These were the kind of people that go to the movies, watch parades, have children, take them to parks, ride in trolley cars, bleed. They had called the general strike but the plans went wrong though the lights did go out that first night, so that it was strange to turn the switch by your bed and see no lamp go on or look out the familiar doorway at the black street empty except for a man with a pistol running. It was strange to go up the countable stairs to the known room and point out of the familiar window the unfamiliar pistol because you believed in elections.

Austria *(cont'd).*
It was strange to be dead where you lived between the desk and the door and the kitchen chair: uncaesarlike, merely dead. Four days of bitter July: ill-led, outnumbered, the radio blaring lies and the six-inch guns and the armoured cars sweeping the square; and the sensible ones gave in and accepted the badge, the armband, the blindfold, and the shining tin truce.

tionalist Socialist demonstrators were greatly exaggerated by foreign correspondents unaccustomed to full-blooded Aryan enthusiasm and the nature of Greek/Nordic pageantry.

Mulqueen at front of second level.

Mulqueen. Correspondence received. From Avery Brundage, President-elect of the American Amateur Athletic Union to the Canadian Olympic Committee: greetings. Frankly, I don't think you have any business to meddle in this question of anti-semitism. The Canadian Olympic Committee is a sports group, organized and pledged to promote clean competition and sportsmanship. Regardless of in what country the Olympic Games are held, there will always be some group, some religion, some race that can register a protest because of the action of some government of that country, past or present. When you let politics creep into your actions, you're in for trouble. Alien agitators would stab our boys in the back by denying them their birthright of competition in international games. To them and their local stooges our athletes reply in modern vernacular: "Oh yeah!" Patriotic sportsmen everywhere are showing the world that they will not be handicapped by subversive influences and malicious propaganda, and will not be made martyrs to a cause not their own. Certain Jews must now understand that they cannot use these games as a weapon. I ask you to remember two things: there never has been a prominent Jewish athlete in history; no nation since ancient Greece has captured the Olympic spirit as has Germany. I know of no reason why Canada should withdraw, and I am speaking on behalf of the younger generation of both our nations when I say: we are all for participation in the 1936 Olympic Games! Sorry I can't be with you in your deliberations. Hope you decide to join us in Berlin. The Minister of Health.

Minister at the front of the second level.

Minister. The duty of the Canadian Olympic Committee is clear. You must not allow yourselves to be deflected by temporal and temporary issues. Berlin is not the issue. 1936 is not the issue. Nor is 1940, nor 1944, nor 1984. The Twenty-First Century is Canada's! and it is to that that you must direct your attention. The rules of the International Olympic Committee permit the inclusion of any conceivable activity. If it is practised in ten countries, six of which agree to compete in it, it becomes an Olympic event. The immediate task of the Canadian Olympic Committee is this: you must determine which are Canada's indigenous events and you must introduce them: first to other countries, then into competition. What are Canada's indigenous events? I hope you do not expect me to answer that question: not today, not here, not tomorrow. Nor do I expect you to. But you must consider it: today, here, and for the multitude of morrows that lie between us and our destiny. That I do expect of you—as does Canada—as, without knowing it, does the world. Of course you must not ignore current events. There has been, is, will be: controversy. And you must respond to it in an athletic and a Canadian manner by beginning your deliberations with a reappraisal of the very nature of Olympic activity. On that point I can be of some assistance. It is my conclusion that the stupidity of the Olympics is its failure to distinguish between Sport and Athletics, and to indulge in the former while expecting the benefits of the latter. The goal of Sport is mastery-of-others; the goal of Athletics is self-mastery. The greater his success in self-mastery, the less frustrated the athlete and the less his need to engage in Sport. It is Canada's destiny to develop a race of athletes of such consummate self-mastery that their need to engage in Sport is forever dead. You may rest assured that the Ministry of Health daily urges the support of your endeavours in the halls of government and the corridors of power.

Voice of Kapek on wand.

Kapek. O Lord, creator of my beautiful Czechoslovakia, to you we need not describe what has befallen us nor how our heads are bowed. Not bowed in shame. We have no cause for shame though struck with an iron hand. We have not been crushed. We have not shown too little courage. Our nation did not lose its honour. It lost only part of its body. We are like the man caught in the cogs of a wheel who feels from the very first and with the most excruciating pain that he is alive, still alive O Lord, we have nothing to fear from the course of world events. We must work among ourselves. We must love each other even more. We must believe that our mission is to make of ourselves a better nation. O Lord, help us to believe it! O Lord, creator of my beautiful Czechoslovakia, we do not pray that we may be avenged. We only pray that you will let none of us yield to despair, for never can a nation be called small whose faith is great enough to build the future. O Lord, accept this prayer from your servant Carl Kapek one month before his death.

Housing commissions, mortgage subsidies, urban renewal—hundreds of millions for the city slums! What about the body slums? Boards of education, programmes of scholarship, institutes of research—art councils, art museums, art centres—the national intellect! the national soul! What about the national physique? It is the challenge of the Canadian Olympic Committee to devise an Olympic Games that will celebrate the new Canadian athlete so that the sons of our sons and the daughters of our daughters, their bodies bent in activities as yet undreamt for tastes hitherto unborn, may look upon your works and say: "They served!"

Mulqueen. The Women's Amateur Sports Programme.

W.A.S.P. at the front of the second level.

W.A.S.P. Mama died when I was little. I knew only governesses—as far as one can know a governess, or cares to. I did not marry. I was not asked. Twice I was close to asking, but Papa would have known. I am—as they used to say—ill-favoured. No deformities: a certain lack of grace. I inherited much from Papa: his estate, his nose. His habit of speaking his mind. When one obtains a certain prominence, lack of frankness is unnecessary. Canada is less than frank. It expected us to care for the minorities but would not tell us who they were. And when we had found them, it had not told them who we were. How could one make plans? And yet plans had to be made. So Papa chose amateur theatrics. I, amateur sport. Sport produces a kind of fame: short-term, to be sure, but enormous. The athlete is unsuited to fame. His youth, his background dispose him to excesses of every kind. How to allow the athlete his celebrity but protect him from involvement in mischievous politics? Amateurism! Amateurism teaches the athlete to accept fame without aggression, victory without arrogance, defeat without surprise. How to protect the amateur from dependence upon a source as complex and various as the one from which he has emerged?—which is to say, the buying public. Patronage! To the recipient of patronage: his satisfactions are personal; his enthusiasms, institutional; his loyalties, national. In a word love—love of self, love of group, love of country. Patronage is love. Therefore, I make the following proposal: if you of the Canadian Olympic Committee will vote to send a Canadian team to Berlin, we will agree to send a Canadian team to Barcelona. When I say we, I mean certain independent sports enthusiasts such as the Women's Amateur Sports Programme. We shall pay their expenses. You have only to guarantee that, upon their return from Spain, you of the Canadian Olympic Committee will not suspend them. I will guarantee that they receive no newspaper coverage. A small team, to be sure: five, perhaps six; Jews in whole or part. With a team in both the pro- and the anti-Olympics I think we shall have fulfilled our responsibility to the Canadian athlete and satisfied him. Ladies and gentlemen of the Canadian Olympic Committee: the athlete's is a universe of exquisites: of micro-seconds, centograms, ohms, ergs and millimeters; on concentrations gathered, of tensions slowly knit; of tempo, balance, focus, thrust! and the taste and pace of pain. The athlete is gifted, sensitive—too gifted, too sensitive to bear responsibility. He must be free. Amateurism makes him free. Amateurism is not a prelude to professionalism but an alternative to it. Which is not to say there shall be no professionals. In Sport the place for professionals is in administration.

Mulqueen, Minister, W.A.S.P. exit.

Voice of Brecht on wand.

Brecht. When the regime ordered that books with dangerous teachings should be burnt and everywhere oxen were forced to draw carts full of books to the funeral pyre, an exiled poet—I, Bertolt Brecht, one of the best—discovered with fury when I studied the list of the burned, that my books had been forgotten. I rushed to my table and wrote to those in power: burn me, I wrote, burn me! Do not treat me in this fashion! Do not leave me out! Have I not always spoken the truth in my books? And now you treat me like a liar! I order you: burn me!

Tecumseh, A Drama

Charles Mair

First published 1886
First production, Riverdale Park, 1971, by Toronto Truck Theatre

Act III, Scene 5
Characters in the excerpt: Prophet, Tarhay, Iena, Mamatee, Braves

Charles Mair (1838 - 1927) was born in Lanark, Ontario. He began to study medicine at Queen's University, but had to leave to work in the family business. At the age of twenty-eight he went to Ottawa, where he became a member of the patriotic Canada First movement. Later, he travelled west and was captured by Riel during the Red River rebellion of 1869. He soon escaped, however, and set about rousing the Orangemen to avenge the death of Thomas Scott who had been executed on Riel's order. After a life of business, writing, government service and adventure, Mair retired in 1921.

Tecumseh was first published in 1886, its writing having been interrupted by Riel's North West rebellion of 1885. The play's uneven blank verse extends for five acts in twenty-eight scenes. It is as dated as a Victorian bathing costume, and just as cumbersome. Amazingly enough, the play, although it appears to us a period piece, a patriotic melodrama in national costume, uses a dramatic device which is fashionable just now: it mixes reportage and propaganda. Perhaps this is why it received two productions in Toronto in 1971, the first by Toronto Truck Theatre, and the second at the Factory Lab under the name of *The Red Revolutionary*.

The hero, Tecumseh, has joined the English under General Brock to resist the American forces commanded by General Harrison in the Anglo-American war of 1812. The action takes place mainly in the forest around the town of Tippecanoe which is controlled by the Prophet, Tecumseh's sinister brother, and in Vincennes, the headquarters of Harrison. In general, Mair's play is faithful to history, although events are condensed somewhat. Tecumseh is portrayed as courageous and as far-sighted as he was in life. By playing on the superstitious credulity of many of the Indians, his evil brother, the Prophet, gains temporary support, but is discredited when his magic is seen to fail. Although this one-eyed magician complicated the plans of Tecumseh for a united Indian nation and really contributed to the failure of the scheme, Mair probably makes him even more of a melodramatic villain than he was in reality. In the play, he is made to play the role of wicked uncle to a niece, Iena, invented by Mair to provide an amorous sub-plot to the military action.

Our excerpt reveals something of this melodramatic aspect of the play. It is a pity that the Prophet, suitably wicked looking with his single gleaming eye, cannot also sport a villain's waxed moustache. Although it is Tecumseh's law which forbids any marriage between redskin and white, it is the Prophet who confronts Iena and Tecumseh's wife, Mamatee, with the news that Iena must submit to the brave, Tarhay, rather than marry the man she loves, the white Lefroy. Actors trying this scene might attempt the following experiment: play the scene through, sending it up deliberately; then play it again, after more careful study, endeavouring to act the roles of Victorian actors playing it straight.

An open space in the forest near the Prophet's Town. A fire of billets burning. War-cries are heard from the town.

Enter the Prophet.

Prophet. My spells do work apace! Shout yourselves hoarse,
  Ye howling ministers by whom I climb!
  For this I've wrought until my weary tongue,
  Blistered with incantation, flags in speech,
  And half declines its office. Every brave,
  Inflamed by charms and oracles, is now
  A vengeful serpent, who will glide ere morn
  To sting the Long-Knife's sleeping camp to death.
  Why should I hesitate? My promises!
  My duty to Tecumseh! What are these
  Compared with duty here? Where I perceive
  A near advantage, there my duty lies;
  Consideration strong which overweighs
  All other reason. Here is Harrison—
  Trapanned to dangerous lodgment for the night—
  Each deep ravine which grooves the prairie's breast
  A channel of approach; each winding creek
  A screen for creeping death. Revenge is sick
  To think of such advantage flung aside.
  For what? To let Tecumseh's greatness grow,
  Who gathers his rich harvest of renown
  Out of the very fields that I have sown!
  By Manitou, I will endure no more!
  Nor, in the rising flood of our affairs,
  Fish like an osprey for this eagle longer.
  But, soft! It is the midnight hour when comes
  Tarhay to claim his bride, *(calls)* Tarhay! Tarhay!

Enter Tarhay with several braves

Tarhay. Tarhay is here!

Prophet.   The Long-Knives die to-night.
  The spirits which do minister to me
  Have breathed this utterance within my ear.
  You know my sacred office cuts me off
  From the immediate leadership in fight.
  My nobler work is in the spirit-world,
  And thence come promises which make us strong.
  Near to the foe I'll keep the Magic Bowl,
  Whilst you, Tarhay, shall lead our warriors on.

Tarhay. I'll lead them; they are wild with eagerness.

But fill my cold and empty cabin first
With light and heat! You know I love your niece,
And have the promise of her hand to-night.

Prophet. She shall be yours! *(To the braves)*
Go bring her here at once—
But, look! Fulfilment of my promise comes
In her own person.

Enter Iena and Mamatee

Welcome, my sweet niece!
You have forestalled my message by these braves,
And come unbidden to your wedding place.

Iena. Uncle! you know my heart is far away—

Prophet. But still your hand is here! this little hand!
(Pulling her forward)

Iena. Dare you enforce a weak and helpless girl,
Who thought to move you by her misery?
Stand back! I have a message for you too.
What means the war-like song, the dance of braves,
And bustle in our town?

Prophet. It means that we
Attack the foe to-night.

Iena. And risk our all?
O that Tecumseh knew! his soul would rush
In arms to intercept you. What! break faith,
And on the hazard of a doubtful strife
Stake his great enterprise and all our lives!
The dying curses of a ruined race
Will wither up your wicked heart for this!

Prophet. False girl! your heart is with our foes;
Your hand I mean to turn to better use.

Iena. Oh, could it turn you from your mad intent
How freely would I give it! Drop this scheme,
Dismiss your frenzied warriors to their beds,
And, if contented with my hand, Tarhay
Can have it here.

Tarhay. I love you, Iena!

Iena. Then must you love what I do! Love our race!
'Tis this love nerves Tecumseh to unite
Its scattered tribes—his fruit of noble toil,
Which you would snatch unripened from his hand
And feed to sour ambition. Touch it not—
Oh, touch it not, Tarhay! and though my heart
Breaks for it, I am yours.

Prophet. His anyway,
Or I am not the Prophet!

Tarhay. For my part
I have no leaning to this rash attempt,
Since Iena consents to be my wife.

Prophet. Shall I be thwarted by a yearning fool!
(aside)
This soft, sleek girl, to outward seeming good,
I know to be a very fiend beneath—
Whose sly affections centre on herself,
And feed the gliding snake within her heart.

Tarhay. I cannot think her so—

Mamatee. She is not so!
There is the snake that creeps among our race,
Whose venomed fangs would bite into our lives,
And poison all our hopes.

Prophet. She is the head—
The very neck of danger to me here,
Which I must break at once! *(Aside)* Tarhay—attend!
I can see dreadful visions in the air;
I can dream awful dreams of life and fate;
I can bring darkness on the heavy earth;
I can fetch shadows from our fathers' graves,
And spectres from the sepulchres of hell.
Who dares dispute with me disputes with death!
Dost hear, Tarhay?

Tarhay and braves cower before the Prophet.

Tarhay. I hear, and will obey.
Spare me! Spare me!

Prophet. As for this foolish girl,
The hand she offers you on one condition,
I give to you upon a better one;
And, since she has no mind to give her heart—
Which, rest assured, is in her body still—
There,—take it at my hands!

Flings Iena violently toward Tarhay, into whose arms she falls fainting, and is then borne away by Mamatee.

(to Tarhay) Go bring the braves to view the Mystic Torch
And belt of Sacred Beans grown from my flesh—
One touch of it makes them invulnerable—
Then creep, like stealthy panthers, on the foe!

Yesterday the Children Were Dancing

Gratien Gélinas

Published in English 1967
First production in English, Prince Edward Island, 1967, at Charlottetown Festival

From Act II, Scene 6
Characters in the excerpt: Andre, Gravel, O'Brien, Nicole

Gratien Gélinas, born in 1909 at Saint-Tite de Champlain in Quebec, was raised and educated in Montreal. When he was a boy he wished to become a priest, as two of his uncles had done. Yet a desire to preach is not the basis of his writing. His art derives rather from comic mimicry and the character monologue. He discovered comic monologues in his teens, and would adapt them to accommodate his own brand of comedy. Then he began to write his own monologues, gradually evolving his famous character, Fridolin.

In the thirties, Gélinas claims, there were only about five people able to earn a living as professional actors in Quebec. But Gélinas managed to get his own radio show, and in 1942 even started a film company. The war put a stop to that. In 1948 he scored a great success with his play *Tit-Coq*, which fulfilled his ambition to write a good play using Canadian characters, the kind of people he knew very well. In the 1950's, Gélinas acquired his own theatre (Montreal's old Gaiety) and called his company La Comédie-Canadienne. He planned to produce only Canadian plays, and this he managed to do for the first three years, by which time writers were turning increasingly to films and television.

In an interview for C.B.C. Radio in 1972, Gélinas asserted that the playwright should forget his message, and give us emotion and a significant, memorable event; he should also reflect our national identity. As an actor and all-round man of the theatre, he does not see drama as primarily written literature. It is an oral art, the written parts being a kind of blueprint for the transaction which occurs between actors and audience. Without actors, theatre could not exist. Without audiences, a presentation would not be a performance so much as a mere rehearsal.

Yesterday the Children Were Dancing vividly enacts the dilemma of the middle-class politics of parliamentary procedure confronted by the agonizing fact of F.L.Q. violence. Of the rebellious young people we encounter in some of the plays represented in this scene-book, André is the most resolute, meticulous, articulate and politically committed. He acts out of a determined political passion and genuine political faith, even if he is misguided. His is by no means a chaotic personality in need of therapy and love. He sees clearly the enormity of his thorough and clever plan, which involves a chain of helpers including his younger brother, and which can ruin his father's political career. He knows that he faces imprisonment and maybe death. From this blend of complex family relationships, and moral and political choices, Gélinas has created a very strong dramatic alloy which proves to be perhaps the most complex and dynamic excerpt in this book.

The setting of our excerpt is the Gravel's living-room in Montreal. The time is 1967. The room is comfortably and tastefully furnished. There must be a telephone on a narrow table behind the sofa which occupies the centre of the room. It is on this telephone that Gravel, a Quebec politician, has been offered a cabinet post in Ottawa by Mr. Pearson in the previous scene. Scene 6 opens after this good news has been received, and immediately after Gravel's joy is reversed by André who delivers the blow which might destroy his father's political career: he reveals that he is leader of a militant group of bomb-planting young separatists, and intends to give himself up to the authorities, as a patriotic gesture of great propaganda value. The confrontation between father and son, and between their two opposing politics, takes place in the presence of O'Brien, Gravel's brother-in-law and partner in the family law practice, and the attractive, forthright Nicole, André's girl friend.

The Gravel's living-room in Montreal. The Present.

The atmosphere is one of elegance and more especially of warmth. The funiture is in good taste, but one feels that a woman of serenity has chosen it less to impress visitors than to assure the relaxation of family and friends. The sofa and chairs are, above all, comfortable. One leaves them regretfully, the way one also leaves the room itself. In the left wall is a fireplace and on the back wall, a bookcase contains a record-player and a discreet liquor-cabinet. In the centre a small vestibule opens onto the unseen part of the ground floor and onto the stairway, which leads to the second floor. On the right wall, a picture-window gives onto the street, which is hidden by curtains and drapes. Behind the sofa, which occupies the centre of the room, a narrow table holds the telephone. A sewing basket, a green plant, some newspapers and magazines—and maybe a set of chessmen somewhere—complete the lived-in atmosphere of the room without cluttering it.

At curtain-rise the characters are in the same positions they occupied at the end of Act One: there has been no lapse in the action.

André *(as he finishes taking off his coat).* All right: shoot! *(to his father)* Your last word was "imbecile." Go on: that's the classic opening for a dialogue with a Separatist.

Gravel *(vehemently).* Yes, an imbecile! Or at least a crackpot. If you're as intelligent as you think, you ought to realize that this blessed violence of yours—which you call patriotism—has already been tried and found wanting pathetically!

André. Yes, a good tool can be misused.

O'Brien. Those very people you're trying to win over to your cause, André . . . don't you understand that the surest way of losing them is to explode bombs that might kill their children in the streets?

Gravel. And for the sake of a fiasco like that, you're ready to rot in jail, as other lunatics are doing right now?

André. You condemn them; but history will judge them on appeal with the objectivity you lack.

Gravel. I have no doubt about the verdict.

André. Nor I.

Gravel. It'll still be clear they were sadly mistaken.

André. In the means used, yes. Like the patriots of 1837. But face it: the cause of this new rebellion is every bit as legitimate as theirs, because it's one and the same.

O'Brien. With this essential difference: those rebels were killing British soldiers, not their defenceless countrymen.

André. We'll see we make as much noise as they did, but without sacrificing lives.

O'Brien. Oh sure! Hell is paved with intentions like that.

Gravel. Go into the prisons and ask the deflated little heroes who planted bombs in letter boxes and armouries if it was their intention to kill one man and maim another for life!

André. As I said, apart from what's happened to you today, my plan took everything into account.

O'Brien. Your plan?

André. Yes. I'll take full responsibility.

Nicole. André . . . won't you tell me what it is? I'm afraid for you.

André. If it's any consolation to you, all right. *(pulling a piece of paper from his pocket)* In tomorrow morning's mail, the news media will get a copy of this manifesto. *(he hands it to Nicole.)* If they publish it without distortion, the public will realize there's no danger to them from our fireworks, and they can even enjoy the fun if they feel like it. *(to Nicole)* Will you read it aloud, please?

Nicole *(reading).* "We are seventeen companions. We represent a cross-section of society: labouring, professional, farming, student; and each of us lives in a different city of the State of Quebec."

André. When they're all identified, they'll be recognized as men with reputations —spotless until then—for integrity, ability and stability. *(He signals Nicole to continue.)*

Nicole *(reading).* "Every night until voting day, one of us, each in his own area, will destroy a symbol of British Imperialism, unconnected with private, commercial or industrial property."

André *(commenting).* "In fact, a work of art as meaningless as Wolfe's monument."

Nicole *(reading).* "In every case the target will be a non-habitable structure, so isolated that its destruction will present no risk to neighbouring buildings or their occupants. Moreover, an expert from among the members of the movement will have determined, with the greatest possible precision, the quantity of dynamite in each bomb, so that . . . "

André *(taking over).* " . . . so that the explosion itself affects nothing but the symbol."

Nicole *(reading).* "In addition—"

André. Listen to this.

Nicole *(reading).* "In addition, the bomb will be of a type never before used, made to explode within forty-five seconds of being positioned—"

André *(running on by memory, insisting).* ". . . a safety catch making it until then as inoffensive as a grenade . . . "

Nicole. "This short-lived bomb will reduce the danger to potential passers-by between priming and detonation, a matter of seconds later."

André. You get the point?

Nicole *(continuing).* "During this brief interval, the companion will retire no further than essential to ensure his own safety, so he may be in a position to divert, by signs or words, any unforeseen traffic headed in the direction of the target."

André. In short every detail of the affair will show clearly that we did everything possible to protect human life. *(to Nicole)* And the last paragraph?

Nicole *(reading).* "Once his mission is accomplished, and if he has not already been arrested on the spot, the companion will add to the protest value of his action that of passive resistance by turning himself in of his own accord. In this way the people of Quebec will realize at once that the sabotage is not the work of a dangerous young punk, as malicious legend would have them believe—"

André *(picking up from memory, and concluding).* ". . . but a young compatriot, in every other way respectful of the established order, and not afraid to face the immediate consequences of his act, a strictly political one arising from deep conviction. *(between his teeth)* Long live Free Quebec!"

Nicole *(laying the manifesto down).* Can you rely on your companions, André?

André. As on myself: I spent the summer choosing them, probably more carefully than they pick a Mountie in Ottawa.

O'Brien. Still, if one of them talked—

Gravel. Only one!

O'Brien. . . . despite your confidence in all of them, your whole infallible scheme would collapse.

André. No one will talk.

Gravel. Oh, the spirit is willing, but . . .

André. Police sticks are very convincing, I know that. If they managed to frighten one of my men, there's only one name he could reveal: mine. The others he doesn't know. I'm the sole person who knows the whole network.

Gravel. And of course, there's no question of you giving in!

André. I'm no braver than the average group-member. That's why I insisted every one of them choose his own replacement, whose name I do not know, and who'd take his place if something unavoidable came up to prevent him accomplishing his mission at the appointed time and place. So even if I were enough of a coward to name every one of them, the plan would still be executed.

O'Brien. By tomorrow—and you know it!—the police will be watching like hawks every possible target.

André. All the way from Hull to the Gaspé? Terrific! Then the world would know that in our lovely French province the reminders of Anglo-Saxon colonialism outnumber the available police.

Gravel *(to André).* All right, you've taken precautions.

André. Every conceivable precaution.

Gravel. But all the same you're using explosives.

André. Well, of course! You know a better way of knocking over a pile of stone? We can hardly go through the streets with a bulldozer.

Gravel. Suppose, despite all your precautions, there was an accident?

André. Then leave your car in the garage. You never know when you'll run over a friend, no matter how good your intentions are.

Gravel. That's idiotic!

O'Brien. André, you're remembering to forget a fine point which you, as a lawyer, can't honestly ignore.

André. I was waiting to hear your objection, dear colleague.

O'Brien. Blaming others won't make it right for you to commit an act the law formally labels a crime.

Gravel. Of course!

André. I'm aware of the law: it's the law of the mightiest, so worried about his own skin he won't grant a political suspect the special rights given him in any really civilized country. It's an abominable law, but it's clear. It stipulates that if you're out to deliver your own people, rightly or wrongly, from degrading serfdom, due process of law—as practised by Her Gracious Majesty's government—tosses you in jail, along with common murderers, prostitutes and pyromaniacs. But of course, it's entirely permissible to spread the benefits of American Imperialism by slaughtering thousands of Vietnamese civilians with the blessing of that very same government!

Gravel. Duck and weave all you like; the fact remains that the law, good or bad, will condemn you; and you can't escape.

André. Who's talking about escape? Me?—the one who's going to turn himself in tonight? Get this: I know what's in store for me. But the honourable federalist judge who'll hand down my sentence from on high will find me looking him straight in the eye.

O'Brien. My poor boy!

André. And he'll be pretty uncomfortable, if the practice of his noble profession hasn't totally atrophied his sense of right and wrong. *(by Nicole, anxious to convince her)* He'll recall that besides the organized justice that makes him condemn me, there's also equity—

Gravel. Equity!

André. Equity, pure and simple—which takes into account the circumstances, the true motives, and plain common sense.

Gravel. My God!

Nicole *(who has taken his hand and kissed it).* Sweetheart, how many eternities will you be away from me? Do you know?

O'Brien *(replying for the unhappy André, who hesitates).* The others'll probably get between six months and a year. But you—if they find out you're the leader, and they doubtless will—

André. I won't hide it.

O'Brien. Then you won't get away with less than two years in prison.

André. That's what I figured.

Nicole *(murmering, heartbroken).* Two years! *(She strokes her cheek with André's hand, choking back tears.)*

Gravel *(going to her).* Yes, two years of liberty lost, maybe more. The rest of his young manhood ruined—altogether apart from the anxiety, the harm and the shame he'll heap on those who love him. And all that to achieve illegally what he could more easily achieve by legitimate means.

André *(between his teeth).* If you follow that trail, I warn you, you'll fall right into a bear trap.

Gravel. Oh sure: this musical-comedy plot of yours is clever enough. But you remind me of those petty crooks who spend as much time and effort organizing a five-dollar robbery as they would earning the same amount of money honestly. What is this masochism that makes you plunge headlong into violence, when our democratic system allows anyone to foster the wildest political theory absolutely legally? Your weeping and wailing like Jeremiah won't convince anyone we're living under a dictatorship. If your Separatist ideas are so terrific, if they're the magic cure for all that ails us, lay them honestly before the voters. Who's stopping you? If the people go along with you, then we'll have to face up to them.

André *(with clenched teeth, waiting till Gravel finishes before he counter-attacks).* Oh yes! It would be so simple! *(imitating a crier)* O come all ye sympathetic fools! The political auction is open. Come with your pennies; dig them out of your piggy banks with a knife; put them down right here beside our fat election kitty and try to match our stakes! Come on, you dear little lambs: fall into our trap and join the game of democracy. We're okay, we've got all the trumps right here in our hand: the police, the army, newspapers, television, radio, liquor, patronage, intimidation, libel, blackmail—and last but not least, the real crusher: beauteous, all-powerful Cash! But play fair, though: no dirty tricks. Violence, physical or verbal, is out: that's our preserve! Because we, the Almighty, will legalize it every time we figure you need a lesson!

Gravel *(leaving him for O'Brien)*. How can you turn off such a Niagara of prejudice?

André *(seizing him again)*. You can't! Because you know damn well that elections in your style democracy aren't won with prayers! Your party, grown fat over a hundred years—where would it be without its lousy treasure chest? Independent parties are poor as church mice—and you know that too. If by some miracle they could ever collect a million bucks to plead their cause, the party in power would come up with ten, twenty, fifty! They only need to tell their backers "Cough up a little or lose the lot!"—and they'd cough up every cent needed. We'd be washed out like so much dirt. And you tell us "No violence"? Then what else do we have to fight with?

O'Brien *(raising his voice for the first time, as he feels the ground give way beneath his feet)*. If you think terrorism is the way to educate this province politically, I warn you: you're heading for catastrophe.

André. Excuse me: a nice distinction, if you don't mind! Terrorism, by definition, breeds terror. But the little garage mechanic, all alone on the Plains of Abraham, who rid the province of an antiquated birdshit target as humiliating for us as Wolfe's monument, Mark II—and then presented himself at police HQ and politely told the constable on duty: "Would you be so kind as to arrest me? I'm the guy who just pulled the job on the Plains." Do you for one second imagine he terrorized the grand old city of Champlain? Why, as this very minute, every Quebecker who still has an ounce of national pride ought to be laughing up his sleeve. And that's only the beginning. Within a week they'll be laying odds in the taverns, in recreation halls, in beauty parlours—trying to guess which corner of the province will have the fireworks display that night. What with the boring election campaign we're getting right now, when they go to the polls there'll be more talk about Independence than there'll be about Federalism!

O'Brien. André, if you're honest, as you claim to be, you'll admit that everything you've said so far shows only that you're ingenious—and that we knew already.

Gravel. Just as we know your motives conform to the somewhat dubious moral code you've coined for yourself.

O'Brien. But you've said nothing yet that might prove your cause a good one.

André. What's the point?

Gravel. But my God, that's the whole question! Any fool can play Don Quixote and go smash his head against windmills.

André *(to Nicole)*. Argue in that vein and they'll drag out every cliché known to man!

Gravel. At a time like this, when communications are drawing the five continents closer together than they've ever been throughout history—

André *(to Nicole)*. Number one!

Gravel. . . . what can you possibly find sensible and inspiring about isolating this province like a medieval ghetto? Why confine your ambitions to Quebec when you have the chance to make your presence felt from one end of this rich country of ours to the other?

André. The grand illusion. Sure! Make our presence felt from Halifax to Victoria, when we can't even take over Montreal! Montreal, the second greatest French city in the world—so they say—where an English population of ten per cent is lord and master of eighty-five per cent of the economy!

The telephone rings and O'Brien answers. Only the end of his reply is audible.

O'Brien. Hello? . . . No, this is O'Brien. . . . We're still waiting for her.

André *(having just had time to draw breath).* Start de-anglicizing Westmount before you send me out to frenchify Assiniboia!

O'Brien *(on the phone).* Where are you? . . . Wait for me, and meanwhile don't do a thing: you might regret it. *(Hangs up. To Gravel)* Roberge. I'm going to the Windsor to stall for time.

Gravel shrugs his shoulders as if to say, "What's the good?"

O'Brien *(stopped by André, who holds him in the passage and looks him straight in the eye).* Rest assured, I am no stool pigeon. *(He disengages himself without being rude.)*

André. You see, the coup would still take place, as I've explained.

O'Brien. And anyway, you'd turn yourself in. I got the point. *(He goes upstage, where he dons his coat and exits during the dialogue following.)*

Gravel *(going to his son).* André, listen to me: I'd believe in Separatism with all my heart too, if I weren't convinced it'd mean economic suicide.

André. That's what you think!

Gravel. After enjoying one of the highest standards of living in the world, Quebec would plunge right into the muck for generations to come . . . with all the foul-up brought on by the withdrawal of foreign capital, inflation, the whole rotten mess.

André *(facing up to him).* You're dead certain of that?

Gravel. Absolutely certain.

André. A reasonable man like you doesn't arrive at absolute certainty just casually, now, on grave issues like that: you have figures, surveys, statistics to support your views? Or would you, too, by any chance, stoop to demagogy, making statements which suit your purpose but no one has proven to date?

Gravel. Look: any economist will tell you that with a population of only six million Quebec could never survive!

André. If the danger is so almighty awful, why not prove it, loud and clear? It's your most resounding objection, the only valid one on the whole. Go right ahead! The problem's been kicking around for half a century. But oh no: you'd never tackle it officially. You'd funk facing the conclusion that a free Quebec could get along every bit as well as Sweden!

Gravel. But Sweden's in a completely different context than Quebec: politically it might as well be on another planet. . . . *(Larry's entrance interrupts him.)*

Overlaid

Robertson Davies

First published 1948
First production, Peterborough, 1946

Characters in the excerpt: Ethel, Pop, Bailey, Radio Voices, Male and Female, Jimmy's voice

Born in 1913 in Thamesville, Ontario, Robertson Davies studied at Upper Canada College, Queen's University and Balliol College, Oxford. He acted at the Old Vic in London, England, and taught at the Old Vic School before returning to Canada, where he has since been a journalist, playwright, novelist and distinguished university teacher.

Overlaid, which won the Ottawa Drama League Prize in 1947, is a concise, vigorous theatrical cartoon of Pop's culture-starved household. It exploits that gentle humour which has been a frequent element in Canadian drama. The role of Pop is a good one for the comic character actor, and though the other characters are quickly and clearly defined, their main function is to serve as foils to Pop's exuberance and his vigorous involvement in the distant world of culture and civilization. This comic theme of the struggle out of philistinism into the world of art anticipates the fuller and more serious treatment it gets in Davies' later plays.

A challenge is offered by this excerpt from the beginning of the play not only in the verve and vigour needed, but also in the precisely correct timing of the radio voices and of the actors' reactions to them. Davies creates a comic contrast between the polite idiom of the radio and the rough and ready vigour of Pop's talk in his shabby, comfortable kitchen. It is worth noticing that Davies does not patronize Pop; indeed, the end of the play reveals a great deal of admiration for him.

The scene is a farmhouse kitchen in rural Canada. It is a cluttered and inconvenient room containing a wood range, a dresser, a kitchen table, a radio and several chairs. There is a door leading to the farmyard and another to the house. A light cord, fitted with a double socket, hangs nakedly from the ceiling; a basket of unironed clothes sits under the table; an ironing board and an electric iron are in the corner and on the top of the range respectively.

As the curtain rises the radio rings with the applause of a great audience. Pop, a farmer of seventy, sitting in a kitchen armchair and wearing an ancient and battered top hat, is applauding also; on his hands he wears white cotton workman's gloves.

Radio Voice. Once again our principals are led on by Mr. Panizzi . . . and they bow. You can hear the rapturous applause of this Saturday matinee audience. *(Sound of applause rises.)*

Pop. Attaboy! Yippee!

Radio Voice. Our lovely Lucia, in her handsome green and gold first-act costume, steps forward to acknowledge a special tribute . . . *(tremendous applause.)*

Pop. Hot dog!

Radio Voice. And now, ladies and gentlemen, we have arrived at the first intermission in this Saturday afternoon performance of *Lucia di Lammermoor,* brought to you from the stage of the Metropolitan Opera House in New York City, and in just a few moments I shall ask the president of our Opera Radio Guild, Mrs. August Belmont, to address you.

Pop. Yay, Miz' Belmont!

Ethel, Pop's daughter, enters; she is a hard-faced woman of forty; she takes the basket of clothes from under the table.

Ethel. Poppa, turn that thing down; I can't hear myself think.

Radio Voice *(female).* Friends of the Opera Guild everywhere . . .

Pop. Quiet, gal; Miz' Belmont's goin' to speak.

Ethel. I don't care who it is. You always turn it up loudest when they're clapping. My head's splitting.

Pop. Leave'er be.

Ethel. Oh, don't be so contrary! *(She turns the radio down to a murmur.)* I've got one of my sick headaches; that racket just goes through and through me like a knife. I've got ironing to do out here. *(She sets up her board from the table to a chair back, and then plugs in her iron, climbing on a chair to reach the central light socket.)*

Pop. Oh no you don't. Bump, bump, bump all through my op'ry. You just wait. Go lie down again. Rest your head.

Ethel. It's got to be done. Can't wait. Plenty to do without waiting till half-past five for that row to be over.

Pop. Row, eh? Say, whose house is this anyways? Mine or your'n?

Ethel. Yours, of course, but I do the work and keep things decent and Jim works the farm. You can't expect to have everything your own way; you know that.

Pop. I'll have this my own way. Now you turn up that radio so's I can hear Miz' Belmont.

Ethel. Oh, don't be so childish! What do you want to hear some society woman in New York for?

Pop. What for? Because she's my kind, that's what for! I'm a member of the Op'ry Radio Guild; paid my three bucks and got a ticket says so. This here Miz' Belmont, she's boss of the Guild. Guess I can hear her if I want!

Ethel. Your kind! Ptuh! *(She tests her iron by spitting on it.)*

Pop. Yes, my kind and no "ptuh" about it neither. Just because you were a schoolmarm before you married a dumb farmer you think you're everybody, don't you? Well, you never had no ear for music, nor no artistic soul. You ain't never been one of the artistic crowd.

Ethel. And you are, I suppose? *(She is now ironing as though she were punishing the clothes, sprinkling and thumping illnaturedly.)*

Pop. Durn right I am! Look at me! I'm at the op'ry, the only fella in this township that is, I betcha. And where's Jim? Layin' out in the barn asleep, though you think he's workin'. And where are you? Layin' on the bed, hatin' the world and feelin' sick, and he thinks you're workin'. You're emotionally understimulated, the both of you—

Ethel. What did you say?

Pop. You heard me good enough.

Ethel. Listen, Poppa. I've stood a good deal from you, but I won't have that kind of talk.

Pop. What's wrong with it?

Ethel. You know, well enough. Emotion, and that. Suppose little Jimmy was to hear?

Pop. Well, what if he does?

Ethel. A child like that? Putting ideas in his head!

Pop. Do him good. Any ideas he gets in this house he'll have to get from me. You and Jim ain't got none. *(He turns up the radio.)*

Radio Voice *(female).* If our lives lack beauty, we are poor indeed. . . .

Ethel. Emotionally understimulated! You were always loose.

Pop. Hey?

Ethel. I know what Mother went through. *(Turns radio down.)*

Pop. Oh, you do, do you? Well, you don't. Your Ma was kinda like you—just as dumb but not as mean.

Ethel. Don't speak so of Mother!

Pop. I knew your Ma better than you did. She worked like a nigger on this farm: we both did. When she wasn't workin' she was up to some religious didoes at the church. Then come forty-five or fifty she broke down and had to have a spell in the bughouse. Never properly got over it. More and more religion: more and more hell-raisin' at home. Folks say I drove her crazy. It's a lie. Emotional undernourishment is what done it, and it'll do the same for you. You an' your sick headaches!

Ethel. Poppa, that's the meanest thing you ever said! You're a wicked old man!

Pop. Yeh, but I'm happy, an' that's more than most of 'em can say' round here. I'm the bohemian set of Smith township, all in one man. Now you let Miz' Belmont speak. *(He turns up the radio: Jimmy's voice, the changing voice of a boy of fourteen, is heard outside.)*

Jimmy. Hey, Maw! Hey, Maw!

Radio Voice. No life to-day need be starved for the fulfilment which the noblest art can give. It is to be had for the taking: great music, great drama . . .

Ethel *(at the door, fondly).* What is it, Lover?

Jimmy. Car comin' in from the road.

Ethel. Do you know whose?

Jimmy. Naw: from town by the looks of it.

Ethel. Well—don't get cold, will you, Lover? *(She closes the door and turns down radio.)*

Pop. Lover! Huh!

Ethel. Well, what about it? He's my own son, isn't he?

Pop. Yeh. Bet you never called Jim "Lover".

Ethel. Of course not. To a grown person it ain't—isn't decent.

Pop. You said ain't!

Ethel. Living with you it's a wonder any of my Normal School sticks to me at all.

Pop. Never could figure why they call them things Normal. Now who's comin' here to bust in on my Saturday afternoon; the one time o' the week when I get a little food for my immortal soul.

Ethel *(from window).* It's that insurance agent from town.

Pop. Aw, him! What's he want?

A loud knock at the door and George Bailey enters; he is a fat man with a frequent, phlegmy laugh.

G.B. Well, well, lots o' snow you got out here, eh? Afternoon, Miz' Cochran. Hi, Grandpop! Holy Gol, what are you doin' in that get-up for Pete sake?

Pop. Awright now, G.B.; awright; say your say and don't be all day over it. I'm busy.

Ethel. Poppa, what a way to talk to a man who's just come in out of the cold. Will you have a cup of tea, Mr. Bailey?

G.B. Sure, thanks, if you got it handy.

Ethel. Right on the stove; always keep some going.

G.B. Now then, Grandpop, what's the big idea? Gettin' ready for an Orange Walk, or something?

Pop. If you got to know, I'm listenin' to the op'ry on the radio. I listen every Saturday afternoon. I'm a paid-up member of the Op'ry Radio Guild, same as Miz' August Belmont. This hat is what's called an op'ry hat, but I guess you wouldn't understand about that.

G.B. *(uproarious).* Holy smoke! And what's the idea of the furnaceman's gloves?

Pop. In New York white gloves for the op'ry are *dee rigger*. That's French for you can't get in without'em.

G.B. *(choking).* Well by gollies, now I seen everything.

Pop. No you ain't: you ain't seen nothin', nor been anywheres. That's what's wrong with you and a lot more like you. Now what do you want?

G.B. Keep your shirt on, Grandpop. I'm here on business: 32096-B Pay Life is finished, washed up, and complete.

Pop. Hey?

G.B. Yep. Now, what d'you want to do with the money?

Pop. What money?

G.B. Your money. Your insurance policy is paid up. You were seventy a couple of days ago, weren't you?

Pop. Yeh.

G.B. Well, then—You got twelve hundred dollars comin' to you.

Pop. Is that right?

G.B. You bet it's right. Didn't you know?

Pop. I'd kinda forgotten.

G.B. Gol, you farmers! I wonder you're not all on relief, the kind of business men you are.

Pop. Aw shut up. I been payin' so long I guess I forgot I was payin' for anything except to save you from honest work. Twelve hundred bucks, eh?

G.B. A cool twelve hundred.

Pop. When do I get it?

G.B. Well, now, just a minute, now. You don't have to take the money.

Pop. Oh, I don't, eh?

G.B. No. There's a couple of options. If you want, we'll give you a hundred dollars a year in twelve equal monthly instalments, for twelve years, and if you die before it's all gone (which you will, o'course) the balance will go to your heirs, minus certain deductions for accounting and adjustment. Or if you'd rather we'll give you two hundred cash and a paid-up policy for a thousand, which would give you a smart burial and leave five or six hundred for Miz' Cochran and Jim.

Ethel. Here's your tea.

G.B. Yeah, thanks. *(Gulps some of it.)* What do you think he ought to do?

Ethel. Well—it's hard to say. With twelve hundred we could make a lot of improvements 'round the farm. I know Jim wants a tractor the worst way. But then, the thousand in the hand after Poppa's called home would certainly be welcome. Of course, we hope that won't be for many years yet.

G.B. Nope. The old codger looks good for a while yet. Still, you know, Grandpop, at your time of life anything can happen.

Pop. Yeh? Well, with all that fat on you, and that laugh you got, you might have a stroke any minute. Ever look at it that way?

G.B. By gollies, you're a card. Ain't he a card, eh? Seventy and smart as a steel trap. A regular card.

Pop. You talk like nobody ever lived to seventy before.

G.B. The average life expectancy for men on farms is sixty-point-two years; you're living on borrowed time, Grandpop.

Pop. Borrowed from who?

G.B. What a card! Borrowed from who, he says. It's just a way of speaking; technical.

Pop. Borrowed from you, I hope.

G.B. Aw now, don't get sore. What do you want to do? Personally I'd advise the two-hundred-down-and-a-thousand-at-death plan. Nice, clean-cut proposition, and fix up for Jim and Miz' Cochran when you're gone.

Pop. I ain't gone yet. I'll take the twelve hundred in cash. Got it on you?

G.B. Eh? No. I can write you a cheque. But are you sure you want it that way?

Pop. Sure I'm sure.

Ethel. What are you up to, Poppa?

Pop. None of your business.

Ethel. He'll let you know on Monday, Mr. Bailey.

Pop. I just told him. You keep out o' this.

Ethel. Poppa and Jim and I'll talk it over to-night. We'll phone you on Monday.

Pop. You and Jim nothin'. I made up my mind.

Ethel. You haven't considered.

Pop. Say, whose money is this? Ain't it my insurance?

Ethel. Didn't you take it out to provide for your family?

Pop. Damned if I remember what I took it out for after all these years. Likely I took it out because some insurance agent bamboozled me into it. Never knew it would bring me in anything.

Ethel. Now, Poppa, you don't want to do anything foolish after all those years of paying the premium. You took out the policy to protect your family and properly speaking it's family money, and the family will decide what to do with it.

Pop. What makes you so sure I'd do somethin' foolish?

Ethel. Well, what would you do?

Pop. I'd go to New York and spend it—that's what.

Ethel. You'd what?

G.B. Go on a tear, eh, Grandpop? By gollies you're a card!

Pop. No, I ain't a card. That's what I'm goin' to do. You can write the cheque right now, and I'll catch the 9.15 into town. I got enough money to get me quite a piece of the ways without cashin' it.

G.B. Go on! You ain't serious?

Pop. Durn right I'm serious.

G.B. You can't do that.

Pop. Why not?

G.B. Because you can't. You don't want to go to New York.

Pop. Who says I don't?

G.B. You don't know nobody there. Where'd you sleep an' eat?

Pop. Hotel.

G.B. Go on!

Ethel. He's just keeping this up to torment me, Mr. Bailey.

Pop. You keep out o' this.

G.B. Lookit, Grandpop—are you serious?

Pop. Say, how often do I have to tell you I'm serious?

G.B. Aw, but lookit—two hundred'll buy you a nice trip if you got to go somewheres.

Pop. Two hundred won't last a week where I'm goin! Gimme the twelve hundred an' make it quick!

G.B. Say lookit—do you know how much twelve hundred dollars is?

Pop. 'Tain't much, but it'll have to do.

G.B. Ain't much! Say lookit, do you know what's wrong with you? You're crazy, that's what! What'd you do in New York with twelve hundred dollars?

Pop *(very calmly and with a full sense of the effect of what he says on Ethel and Bailey).* I'll tell you what I'd do, since you're so nosey: I'd get some stylish clothes, and I'd go into one o' these restrunts, and I'd order vittles you never heard of —better'n the burnt truck Ethel calls food—and I'd get a bottle o' wine—cost a dollar, maybe two—and drink it all, and then I'd mosey along to the Metropolitan Opera House and I'd buy me a seat right down beside the trap-drummer, and there I'd sit an' listen, and holler and hoot and raise hell whenever I liked the music, an' throw bookies to the gals, an' wink at the chorus, and when it was over I'd go to one o' these here night-clubs an' eat some more, an' drink whisky, and watch the gals that take off their clothes—every last dud, kinda slow an' divilish till they're bare-naked—an' maybe I'd give one o' em fifty bucks for her brazeer

Ethel *(scandalized).* Poppa!

G.B. Jeepers!

Ethel. You carnal man!

Pop. An' then I'd step along Park Avenoo, an' I'd go right up to the door, an' I'd say, "Is this where Miz' August Belmont lives?" an' the coon would say, "Yes-siree!" an' I'd say, "Tell her one o' the Op'ry Guild gang from up in Canada is here, an' how'd she like to talk over things—"

G.B. Say listen, Grandpop: you're nuts.

Ethel. He must be. Mother was like that at the last, you know.

Pop. She was not: your Ma used to think the Baptist preacher was chasin' her to cut the buttons off her boots, but that was as far as she got. She never had the gumption to pump up a real good dream. Emotional undernourishment: that was what ailed your Ma.

Ethel. There you go again! He's been talking that indecent stuff all afternoon.

Pop. 'Tain't indecent. It's the truth. No food for your immortal souls—that's what ails everybody 'round here—little, shriveled-up, peanut-size souls. *(He turns up the radio with a jerk.)*

Radio Voice *(blaring)* . . . render life gracious with the boon of art . . . .

Ethel *(turning radio down).* Is that what your soul feeds on? Restrunts with shameless women in 'em?

Pop. Yeah, an' music an' booze an' good food an' high-toned conversation—all the things a man can't get here because everybody's too damn dumb to know they're alive. Why do you think so many people go to the bughouse around here, anyways? Because they've starved an' tormented their souls, that's why! Because they're against God an' don't know it, that's why!

Ethel. That's blasphemous!

Pop. It ain't blasphemous! They try to make God in their own little image an' they can't do it same as you can't catch Niagara Falls in a teacup. God likes music an' naked women an' I'm happy to follow his example.

Ethel *(shrieks in outrage).* Eeeeeek!

G.B. *(on firm moral ground at last).* That'll do now! That'll just do o' that! I ain't goin' to listen to no such smut: I got a kiddy at home not three yet! Do you think I'm goin' to give you twelve hundred dollars for that kind o' thing? It wouldn't be business ethics! Say, you better look out I don't report this to the Ministerial Alliance! They'd tell you where you got off, darn soon!

Pop. You mean you won't give me the money?

G.B. Naw!

Pop. You want me to have to write to head office an' ask why?

G.B. I'll tell 'em. Unsound mind, that's why.

Pop. What's your proof?

G.B. You just say what you said about God to any doctor, that's all.

Pop. Yeah, but if I don't?

G.B. Well—

Pop. You'd look kinda silly, wouldn't you?

G.B. Now lookit—

Pop. Would it cost you the agency, do you think?

G.B. Aw, now lookit here—

Pop. A libel suit'd come pretty dear to your company, anyways.

G.B. Libel?

Pop. Libellous to say a man's crazy.

G.B. Miz' Cochran would back me up.

Pop. Serious thing, tryin' to put a man in the bughouse just when he gets some money. Look bad in court.

G.B. *(deflated).* Aw, have it your own way. I'll write you a cheque. *(He sits at the table and does so.)*

Pop. Make it nice an' plain, Now. *(He turns up the radio.)*

Radio Voice *(male, again).* You have been listening to Mrs. August Belmont, president of the Metropolitan Opera Guild, in one of the series of intermission talks which is a regular feature of this Saturday afternoon broadcast. And now to give you a brief outline of Act II of Gaetano Donizetti's romantic masterwork, *Lucia di Lammermoor:* the curtain rises to disclose the magnificent hall of Sir Henry Ashton's castle. Norman (played this afternoon by the American baritone Elmer Backhouse) tells Sir Henry (Mr. Dudelsack) that he need have no fear that Lucy will offer opposition to the proposed marriage with Lord Arthur Bucklaw (played this afternoon by Listino di Prezzi) as her letters to Edgar (Mr. Posaun in to-day's performance) have been intercepted and forgeries substituted for them which will leave no doubt of his faithlessness. At this point Lucia (Miss Fognatura) enters (in a gown of greenish-blue taffeta relieved by cerise gussets and a fichu) to a delicately orchestrated passage for wind and strings. Then, supported entirely by wind, Lucy tells her brother that her hand is promised to another, whereupon he produces the forged letters. "The papers," she cries: "La lettera, mio Dio!" whereupon follows a lively upward rush of brass. . . .

G.B. *(during the foregoing).* Here. Well, g'day, Miz' Cochran. *(He listens to the radio ecstasies.)* Cheest! *(He goes out.)*

Riel: A Play in Two Parts
John Coulter

Published 1962
First production Toronto, 1950, by New Play Society

Part I, Scene 11
Characters in the excerpt: Riel, Tache, O'Donoghue, François, Guard, Crowd

    John Coulter was born in Belfast in 1888. He studied art in Ireland and England. With Middleton Murray he co-edited the *New Adelphi* for three years until 1930. He then joined the B.B.C., coming to Canada not long after in the early 1930's. He has written several works on Irish themes, including the libretto for the radio opera, *Deirdre of the Sorrows* (1944) with music by Healey Willan. He has also written poetry and a short biography of Churchill which was adapted for the stage as *Mr. Churchill of England* (1944). This biography is written in a manner which Coulter called living-newspaper technique. This manner also underlies the dramatic method of Coulter's plays about another historical figure, Louis Riel. Both *Riel* (1962) and *The Trial of Louis Riel* (1968) owe a great deal to documentary techniques.
    Our excerpt from *Riel* is set in a room within Fort Garry sometime in 1869-1870. Its action covers a critical point and reversal in Riel's career as a rebel. It calls for a considerable range of acting effects: the rhetoric of the leader; the intimacy of a man talking to his God; the humility of a leader talking to a priest; the revelation of a man's inner thought; and the ancient device of the messenger speech, represented here in the words of O'Donoghue and François.

As the light comes up, there is applause from a group of people, Riel's supporters: members of the Council, volunteers—but neither O'Donoghue nor François is among them. They are gathered in a room at Fort Garry, and they stand listening to Riel, who now wears a formal black frock coat, with a "Gladstone" wide-wing collar. He carries a silk tall-hat in his hands. But he is wearing moccasins. Tache hovers in the background, listening with anxious attention. Something is affecting Riel. In his voice there is evidence of feeling controlled only with difficulty. This becomes increasingly noticeable as he proceeds.

Riel. So, we have prepared a reception. A great reception. To celebrate the setting-up of this new Province . . . in Confederation. And to honour the arrival, here, of the first *(He hesitates.)* Governor . . . with Colonel Wolseley and his troops. We shall fire a salute of cannon, and provide an escort of as many horsemen as we can muster. I have sent forward my . . . personal . . . respects . . . to . . . Governor Archibald. *(This is received with dissenting cries:* "No!" "No!" "We want you!" "Riel for Governor!" "Governor Riel!" *Riel cuts in.)* No, no, no. I thank you but it is not my wish. *(With sudden sharp emphasis)* It is not my wish to be Governor! *(Pause. He recovers himself. Then, continues quietly.)* I beg you, please. You know I have said always I wish to have power only till I can hand it on. For the best interests of religion and of you my own people here. Now, it is the time to . . . hand on . . . *(He stops abruptly. Sways. Steadies himself.)* That is all. I thank you. Please go now.

They are puzzled and murmur in concern, but they bow and file out. When they have gone, Riel slumps. Tache comes to him, very concerned.

Tache. Monsieur! Monsieur Riel! What is it?

Riel. Nothing, nothing, I am nothing.

Tache. But at this moment—of your victory!

Riel. Victory. *(with sudden vehemence.)* He is a fine man Archibald!

This non sequitur and the violence of it strikes Tache, but he is unsure of the import.

Tache. Yes. Yes.

Riel *(fiercely).* A fine man!

Tache. I pray he may prove so.

Riel crushes his silk hat and tosses it aside. He is very agitated. Tache is horrified. Riel drops to his knees.

Riel. Will you bless me, will you bless me?

Tache. Yes, my son, yes.

Riel. I will say a prayer, may I say a prayer?

Tache. What prayer?

Riel *(crying out).* Oh my Father, help me! Help me—to —accept—endure—this.

Tache *(gently).* You may say that prayer.

Riel. If this be thy will. According to the views of thy Providence—which are beautiful and without measure.

There is a loud scuffling and hullabaloo. O'Donoghue is trying to break in and an armed guard is trying to prevent him.

Voice of Guard. You can not. You can not go in. We have orders.

Voice of O'Donoghue *(simultaneously).* I must! I must go in! Out of my way! It's life or death!

O'Donoghue forces his way in, left, standing off the Guard. The guard retires and O'Donoghue comes excitedly forward. Riel rises and with Tache he turns on O'Donoghue with shock and resentment.

Riel. O'Donoghue!

Tache. Mr. O'Donoghue!

Riel. How dare you. . . .

Tache. What is the meaning. . . .

O'Donoghue. Perfidy. In one word—perfidy.

Riel *and* **Tache.** Perfidy?

O'Donoghue. The old, old story. I warned you. Wolseley! The British soldiers! The Orangemen volunteers! They're here. A few hours march. We could have stopped them. Cut them in pieces. But it's too late. . . . There are a dozen strategic points where we could have *(He shouts.)* decimated them! And the Fenians would have helped.

Riel. They are against the Church the Fenians.

O'Donoghue. Nonsense, nonsense, that old idiotic lie.

Tache. It's neither nonsense nor a lie—the Fenians are a secret society and as such banned by the Church.

O'Donoghue. All right, all right, all right, welcome the Orangemen. Welcome Wolseley. He'll spring his steel trap on you while you welcome him.

Tache. Mr. O'Donoghue, you are grievously mistaken. Colonel Wolseley has precise instructions, from London and Ottawa.

O'Donoghue. He's on his own thousands of miles from London and Ottawa. . .

Tache. He must obey instructions.

O'Donoghue. He'll do what he wants to do out here and square it after with— instructions.

Tache. We will not argue. You will please not go further.

O'Donoghue. I must.

Tache. In that case I am not prepared to listen. *(He turns pointedly away.)* Monsieur Riel, you have the assurances of the ministers and my personal assurance. Count on my presence and support when the Colonel and Governor Archibald arrive.

Riel. Thank you, Monseigneur.

He bows as Tache goes out, left.

O'Donoghue. Oh, Riel you *are* a fool! *(Riel merely turns away.)* Listen. . . .

Riel *(listlessly).* I have the Proclamation of Wolseley, signed by himself. *(He produces it and prepares to read.)*

O'Donoghue *(regarding it with impatient scepticism).* Proclamation! That he's coming here to grab the land, and fight to keep it for Macdonald's immigrants.

Riel *(reading).* "My mission is one of peace. . . . "

O'Donoghue. Of course, of course, the old, old trick.

Riel. "The forces I have the honour of commanding will enter your Province representing no party, either in religion or politics. . . . "

O'Donoghue. No party! His Orangemen no party, it makes me laugh!

Riel. "We will afford equal protection to the lives and property of all races and creeds. . . . "

O'Donoghue. Equal protection no protection, nothing equal to nothing. The old perfidious game. Soothe them with syrup. Get their confidence. Then—pounce.

Riel *(without conviction).* I will not believe this.

The scene begins to darken.

O'Donoghue. Riel you *do* believe it. That's what's eating your heart. *(Riel turns away and sits on the chair.)* Why do you *want* this, to be trapped! *(Sure he has a clue.)* Look at him! Look! The noble patriot, betrayed! The tragic man! *(Their eyes meet. Riel says nothing. O'Donoghue closes in.)* The Orangemen came a thousand miles to have your blood—they'll have your blood and march back with your battered head mounted for trophy on an Orange drum. *(Slight pause. Finally, exasperated past bearing, he shouts.)* Why do you sit there in a daze—waiting for them to strike! Could Wolseley stop his Orangemen even if he wanted to? *(Himself almost hysterical.)* Riel! *(No response. Giving it up.)* All right, you want it and you won't have long to wait.

The Guard has come in from the left.

Guard. Monsieur Riel. François is here.

Riel rises.

Riel. Bring him. *(The Guard goes to bring François. To O'Donoghue.)* I sent François to find out.

O'Donoghue. To spy.

Riel. Now I will talk to him—please, alone.

O'Donoghue. When Wolseley comes count on my presence too, in support—but with my gun.

O'Donoghue goes quickly out, right, as François enters, left. François is a little out of breath, dishevelled, wet and mud-bespattered. He is very agitated.

Riel. You travelled fast.

François. The news. It could not wait.

Riel. Tell me.

François. The Colonel Wolseley, already he takes prisoners.

Riel. Prisoners?

François. The folks who went there from Fort Garry. To see him come. To shout Brava.

Riel. He seized them? *(François nods in assent.)* He seized these unarmed folk?

François. Ya. Ya.

A slight pause. Riel steadies himself.

Riel. What more, François?

François. I saw many things. I did not like what I saw. The soldiers. The *volunteers*. They shout. They shake the fist. They say, "There will be some hangings in Fort Garry! Some French will hang."

Riel. You heard this?

François. And always they talk of Scott. Revenge for Scott. They say. . . . *(He hesitates.)* Pardon, Monsieur Riel. I tell only what they say. . . .

Riel. What?

François. "Monsieur Riel he will be first to hang, tomorrow."

Riel. François, I was prepared to welcome them.

François. They sing a song, "We'll hang him up the river. . . . "

Riel. Please, it is enough. François I have one question. The answer to it will tell, everything. *(Carefully.)* The Governor—Archibald. Is he in camp with Wolseley? Does he come here with Wolseley?

François. This I know. He is not with them. He does not come for many days.

Riel *(a slight pause. Then quietly, as to himself.)* Then it is—perfidy. *(Pause. He reflects. Then suddenly he seizes the Proclamation, tears it in two and flings it on the floor. He shouts.)* Proclamation! Perfidy! *(He makes a gesture of contempt, then turns briskly to François.)* Where do they camp tonight?

François. At Grenouillière.

Riel. I will go there.

François. Monsieur Riel!

Riel. Now. At once. I will make sure.

François. If they take you!

Riel *(with pistol).* They will not take me.

François. It pours rain. It pours now, everywhere. Much rain! Everywhere it will be dark, dark.

The scene is now almost dark.

Riel. Dark, dark everywhere! Come, François.

They go, quickly.

The Trial of Louis Riel

John Coulter

Published 1968
First performance, Regina, 1967

Characters in the excerpt: Counsel for Defence, Crown Counsel, Marceaux, Nolin, Riel, Judge

The Trial of Louis Riel is a companion piece to Coulter's earlier play, *Riel* (for biographical and other details see p. 000). Like its forerunner it is a type of documentary drama. We witness a rather orthodox, highly realistic rendering of Riel's trial for high treason in 1885. Dramatic tension is achieved by two climaxes: Riel's outburst denying the madness his defence counsel attributes to him; and the return of the jury with their verdict, which is followed by Riel's lyrical prayer and the Judge's sentence. The play presents the quiet affirmation of a man who has been both acclaimed as a hero and condemned as a traitor, but who has managed in the face of death itself to preserve his own human dignity and integrity.

The excerpt here offers the interesting challenge of a passage of bilingual cross-examination. The scene is the courtroom at Regina where Riel was tried and sentenced to death.

Defence. Did the prisoner ever tell you he considered himself a prophet?

Marceaux. Le prisonnier vous a-t-il jamais dit qu'il se considérait comme un prophète?

Nolin. Oui, il me l'a dit. Un soir, son ventre fit un bruit. Il m'a demandé si je l'avais entendu. . . .

Marceaux. Yes he did. One evening he had a rumbling in his bowels. He asked me did I hear that. . . .

Nolin. J'ai répondu oui et il m'a dit, "Ça, c'était l'Esprit de dieu. . . . "

Marceaux. I said yes, and he said, "That was the Spirit of God. . . . "

Nolin. "Qui communiquait avec moi par l'intermédiare de mon foie."

Marceaux. "Communicating with me through my liver."

Nolin. Il disait que Dieu lui parlait par l'intermédiare de toutes les parties de son corps.

Marceaux. He said God spoke to him through every part of his body.

Defence. You mentioned a book the prisoner had written and which he showed you. . . .

Marceaux. Vous avez fait allusion à un livre que le prisonnier avait écrit et qu'il vous avait montré. . . .

Defence. Did you notice anything unusual or extraordinary about the book?

Marceaux. Avez-vous rien remarqué d'inhabituel ou d'extraordinaire dans ce livre?

Nolin. Non. Mais Riel disait qu'il l'avait écrit avec du sang de bison.

Marceaux. No. But Riel said it was written with buffalo blood.

Defence. With buffalo blood?

Marceaux. Du sang de bison?

Nolin. C'est ce qu'il a dit.

Marceaux. That's what he said.

Defence. Did he tell you what he intended to do with the Northwest when he was in control?

Marceaux. Vous a-t-il dit ce qu'il comptait faire du Nord-Ouest quand il en aurait la maîtrise?

Nolin. Il disait qu'il le diviserait et qu'il en donnerait des morceaux à diverses nationalités européennes. . . .

Marceuax. He said he would divide it and give portions to various European nationalities. . . .

Nolin. Immigrants. Il disait qu'il allait donner l'Ontario à l'Irlande et qu'il allait laisser aux Ontariens le soin de s'occuper de leurs orangistes.

Marceaux. Immigrants. He said he would give Ontario to Ireland and let *them* worry about their Orangemen themselves.

Laughter in court. Suppressed. Riel can control himself no longer. He gets excitedly to his feet.

Riel. Your Honour, would you permit me. . . .

Judge *(surprised).* Eh? What?

Riel. I have some questions. . . .

Judge. No, no. At the proper time.

Riel. Now. Now.

Judge. You will be given every opportunity.

Riel. Is there any legal way I could be allowed to speak now?

Judge. To speak!

Riel. To ask some questions.

Judge. You should suggest any questions to your counsel.

Riel *(urgent).* Do you allow me to speak?

Judge. Oh, look here, look here. . . .

Riel. My life is at stake. I have some observations. *(Flourishes notes he's been taking.)* Some questions to ask this witness.

Defence *(suppressing indignation).* Your honour, I don't think this is the proper time.

Riel. Before this man leaves the witness box. . . .

Judge. I agree it is not the proper time. *(Riel reluctantly sits down.)*

Defence. I think it necessary the prisoner should thoroughly understand. Anything done in his behalf in this case must be done through his counsel.

Judge. The statute of High Treason states that a prisoner can defend himself personally. . . .

Defence. Or by Counsel. But when Counsel has once been accepted. . . . *(Riel is on his feet again.)*

Riel. Your Honour, this case comes to be extraordinary. The Crown are trying to show that I am guilty. It is their duty. My Counsel, my good friends and lawyers whom I respect, are trying to show I am insane. It is their line of defence. I reject it. I indignantly deny that I am insane.

Defence *(trying to break in).* Your Honour. . . .

Riel *(not giving way).* I am not insane! I declare that in rousing and leading my people against cynical disregard and neglect by Ottawa. . . .

Judge. Stop! You must stop!

Riel. The chance to ask important questions of this witness is slipping by. My good Counsel does not know this man. Counsel is not from this part of the country and does not understand our ways, and so. . . .

Judge. I have said you must stop. Stop! Obey!

Riel. I will obey the Court. But I repeat my life and honour are at stake. If this man. . . .

Judge *(peremptory).* Stop at once! *(Riel sits down.)*

Crown *(rising. Bland. Smiling and soothing).* Your Honour, the prosecution does not object to the prisoner putting questions to the witness.

Defence. We do, your Honour. The prisoner is obstructing the proper management of his case and he must not. I submit he not be allowed to interfere. . . .

Judge. Isn't that a matter between yourself and your client?

Defence. I don't presume to argue with the court. But if we are to continue the case the prisoner must be made to abandon his attitude.

Riel *(rising again).* I cannot abandon my dignity. Here I have to defend myself against the accusation of high treason, or allow the plea that I am insane and consent to the animal life of an asylum. I don't care much about animal life in or out of an asylum, if it does not carry with it the moral existence of an intellectual being in full and sane possession of his faculties.

Judge. Stop now! No more! Stop!

Riel *(beaten. Despairing. Sits down).* Yes, your Honour.

Crown. I think, your Honour, that will be the last witness for the Crown.

A Play on Words

Lister Sinclair

Published 1948
First broadcast 1944, by C.B.C. Radio

Characters in the excerpt: Announcer, Narrator, Discusser, Greek, Roman, Poet, Various Voices Male and Female

Lister Sinclair was born in Bombay, India, in 1921. He attended St. Paul's School in London, England, and later took his B.A. at the University of British Columbia. He then taught Mathematics at the University of Toronto from 1942-1944, obtaining his M.A. in Mathematics there in 1945. Since 1942 he has written and acted for C.B.C. He has worked as a music critic and as a teacher at the Academy of Radio Arts, Toronto. He is a frequent contributor to journals and his dramatic work has won him various important awards. A distinguished figure in Canadian broadcasting, Lister Sinclair is executive vice-president of C.B.C. as well as being in charge of English and French-language programs and special services.

A Play On Words, an early work, was first performed as part of the Stage 45 series produced and directed for C.B.C. by Andrew Allan. It was also translated into French and put out on the French network of C.B.C. It is a seemingly abstract play which avoids story and character development in order to put over a propaganda message against racial prejudice and political intolerance in a very straightforward way. The message, though, is conveyed by means of light humour, quick changes of mood and a playful approach to language that gently reminds us that the decay and debasement of language is also an indication of various threats to the quality of life ranging from modern advertising to the dangerous passions which lead to such wars as the one which was still raging when the play was first broadcast.

Our excerpt is taken from the beginning of the play, and calls for a relaxed lightness of tone achieved through very careful timing and slickness in the changes from one voice to another. All cues must be taken up with complete smoothness and attention must be given to every little touch of satire.

Sound: one stroke on a small clear bell.

Narrator *(speaking in a leisurely, conversational manner).* This program is a play on words. It has to do with the sounds men make with their throats and tongues, and with the strange way in which men from different countries make different sounds to express the same meaning:

English. You see, my wife doesn't understand me.

French. Tu vois, ma femme ne me comprend pas.

Gaelic. Mata, cha'n'eil mo bhean 'gam thuigeadh.

German. Du siehst, meine Frau versteht mich nicht.

Spanish. Pues, mi esposa no me coprende.

Their intonations match.

Narrator. And so on; for hundreds of different languages, all made up of words. The programme also has to do with various little marks on paper, papyrus, tablets of wax, and other materials; with various similar marks carved on slabs of stone or in caves, or chiselled up outside temples, or scrawled up in telephone booths. In fact, as we said, this is a *Play on Words!*

Music: Opening cue . . . up and BG.

Announcer. Opening Announcement.

Music: Up to finish.

Discusser *(briskly).* Words are kept in a storehouse, called a dictionary, and when we borrow these words and arrange them in various orders, the result is Language.

Narrator. This word business goes back a long, long way.

Music: The weight of history.

Narrator *(This is going to be a treat!)* Back to One Million B.C.!

Discusser. We start at the Present Day.

Music: Continues beneath, reflecting the changing periods.

Joe. Lookit, honey, I just got a forty-eight! What say we go and get hitched?

Narrator. Past the upholstered opulence of the Victorian Era.

Edward. With your parents' very gracious permission, I have the honour, dear madam, to solicit the rare privilege of your hand in marriage.

Discusser. Back we go, past the gallant days of the eighteenth century, and the rollicking romanticism of the Elizabethans.

Robin. Come live with me, my love, and you shall be my bonny bride!

Narrator. Past the dumb, tortured days of the dark ages we go, and past the Glory that was Greece; past the Grandeur that was Rome, too, for that matter; even past the dignified days of Ancient Egypt where men lived this life as if they were already in the next one.

Discusser. We leave the Pharaohs far behind, and also the Emperors of China; and pass by the days when Nineveh was young, and Ur of the Chaldees was starting out as a village, and as for Tyre and Sidon and Babylon and Troy; well, they hadn't even been *thought* of!

Back, back we go across the illimitable arena of eternity, until at last:

Music: Comes to a crashing climax!

A Booming Voice. One Million B.C.! *(pause).*

Narrator *(slowly).* One Million B.C. *(pause).*

Music: Slow oily theme on solo bass clarinet starts; when it is established:

Narrator. One million B.C., when man was just an infant, and all the world was young. One Million B.C.

Music: Stops with an abrupt tweak!

Narrator *(swiftly).* What does it make *you* think of?

Betsy Co-Ed. One Million B.C.? Why Victor Mature, of course, and *Men:* with long, straight legs, and short curly hair!

Discusser. Too bad! Go along to a museum some time, and take a look at one of those early men. They had long straight hair, and short curly legs!

Narrator *(informatively).* The well dressed man wore furs on his back and hair on his chest. Instead of joining a club, he carried one. When he wanted to propose to some prehistoric lady, he would take his club in one hand, and grab her hair with the other; firmly, of course, but not necessarily gently. Then he would pull; like this:

Piltdown Woman *(a genuine prehistoric screech.)* ! ! !

Narrator. And then if she needed a little more persuasion, he would just touch her lightly behind the ear with his club. Like this:

Piltdown Woman *(another screech during which:)* !!!

Sound: Clunk! There is silence.

Discusser. But Prehistoric Man was All Right. He discovered a lot of things that you and I couldn't do without today.

Narrator. Like wheels, and ships and fire.

Discusser. And words! Yes, he discovered words. We aren't sure how he did it. Probably not deliberately at all. Probably *not* like this:

A Cro-Magnon Ph.D. I'm getting fed up with calling this thing. "Long-bit-wood-with-one-end-sharpened-sticking-into-people-for-the-use-of". I know what I'll call it! A Spear! That's *much* better! Spear!

Narrator. No, no; far more likely he noticed the noise people made when the wooden things were stuck into them:

An Impaled Neanderthaler. Ouch!!

Narrator. Which caused the wooden thing to be called an "Ouch."

Discusser. But how did "Ouch" turn into "Spear"? After all, the word is spear nowadays.

Narrator *(evasively). That* . . . nobody knows. But, remember that was one million years ago. You get a lot of people talking about things with their mouths full, and lisping and stuttering and so forth for one million years, and anything can happen! In any case, whether we like it or not, that's the theory *the Scientists* like!

Discusser *(conclusively).* So that's how it all started

Sound: "Pong".

Narrator. But let's get down to the words *we* use *today.* Let's forget about the other people!

Discusser. Can't be done. You see, most of the words *we* use *today* are stolen, or as the philologists say "borrowed" from other people. Take two common enough words: Polite and Idiot. We all know how they've ended up, but can anybody tell you how they started out?

Greek. I can tell you!

Music: States a Greek theme; then continues beneath to voice.

Discusser. And who are you, sir?

Greek. I am an Ancient Greek. Polite and Idiot began their careers in Ancient Greece. It may surprise you to hear this, but they were in fact Political Terms. In Ancient Greece, it was held to be the clear duty of every citizen to take an active part in politics; not electioneering, or party promotion, or vote grubbing, but true politics; the Science and Art of Government. A man who did his duty in this respect was said to be "Polites", a citizen: while a man who did not do his duty was said to be "Idiotes".

Narrator. But how does this bear on their meaning today?

Greek. Clearly on the one hand, a man who does his duty to his fellows is a thoroughly civilized individual, and so Polite; whereas, on the other hand a person who did not do his duty rapidly came to be regarded as a person who was mentally incapable of doing his duty, and so an Idiot.

Music: Ceases with the voice.

Narrator. But how in the world did the political terms of Ancient Greece come to be a part of English? How did Greek words get to England?

Roman. I expect I brought them with me.

Discusser. Who are you, sir?

Roman. I am a Roman Centurion.

Music: States Roman theme. Continues underneath.

Roman. I sailed with Julius Caesar. We sailed with him to Britain, we Romans and brought with us the trappings of civilization: Roads, Law and Language. When we left, hundred of years later, we left behind us forever, our roads that always led to Rome, mother of cities; our Law, mother of Laws; and our Language, Latin, mother of Languages. Every language in Europe carries the imprint of Latin; English is solidly founded on our mellifluous Latin tongue. It is our words that the orator uses; and the poet:

Music: Pauses.

Poet. "Will all great Neptune's ocean wash this blood
Clean from my hands? No, this my hand will rather
The multitudinous seas incarnadine!"

Roman. There they are, the rolling, majestic syllables of Imperial Rome; the poet will translate that last line into Saxon for us, if you please. It shows the contrast:

Poet. "Will all great Neptune's ocean wash this blood
Clean from my hands? No, this my hand will rather
The multitudinous seas incarnadine.
Making the green one red!"

Music: Closes the sequence.

Roman. You see? There it is in Saxon: "Making the green one red".

Narrator. Indeed, the Saxon is not half so couth. Remember "Alice Through the Looking Glass". Remember what Humpty-Dumpty used to say?

Humpty-Dumpty. Impenetrability! That's what I say!

Discusser. Yes, indeed; there's a rollicking Roman remark. Let's have that in Saxon, please, Humpty-Dumpty.

Humpty-Dumpty. Un-go-through-some-ness! That's what I say!

Narrator. We certainly owe a lot of music to the Romans. But you were explaining to us just how the English managed to get hold of Greek words.

Music: Again to Roman Music.

Roman. We brought them with *us;* Greek has always been the language of culture and philosophy; all cultured Romans spoke Greek, and we left a residue of Greek with our own Latin. Even today the language of Science is still taken from Greek:

Various Voices. Philosophy. Psychology. Telescope. Microscope. Heliograph. Telephone. Seismograph. Spectrohelioscope. Electroencephalograph.

Music: Ends the catalogue.

Discusser. Well, we could carry on like this all night, of course, for practically every language under the sun has chipped in its two bits worth to help build up modern English. Once upon a time, we must remember, England was a much invaded little Island. Remember that last invasion?

Music: A doleful alarum of trumpets.

Proclaimer. Duke William of Normandy has landed at Hastings!

Music: A stern alarum of trumpets.

Discusser. William the Conqueror, 1066. And with him came his language, the haughty Norman French. You still find it in mottoes—and in the Houses of Parliament! When a bill is passed by Parliament, the Royal assent is given in the words:

Assent. Le Roy le veult!

Discusser. Le Roy le veult! Norman French—the King wishes it; and in fact when the King dies, the Herald tells the people the news in the age-old language of chivalry: Norman French.

Music: Flourish!!

Herald. Le Roy est mort! Vive le Roy!

Music: Flourish!!

Discusser. The King is dead; long live the King! But they still say it in Norman French!

Narrator *(impatiently).* And Norman French comes from Latin, and we're already done with Latin.

Discusser *(conclusively).* So much for the History of the words we use!

Does Anybody Here Know Denny?

Sandy Stern

Published 1970
Televised 1969

Characters in the excerpt: Denny, Evelyn, Carol, Corwin, Art, Krantz, Carson

Sandy Stern is a successful writer of scripts for the mass media in North America. He has written for such programs as *The Bold Ones, Wojeck, Ironside* and *All in the Family.*

Does Anybody Here Know Denny? is the story of an heiress who rebels against her family and their *mores* after the death of her father. Denny's revolt arises partly from her own wild and reckless nature, and partly as a means of satisfying her desire for excitement. It is also a plea for Corwin's love. Her aggressive use of wealth and her directness amount to a technique for penetrating people's masks, getting revenge against hypocrisy, and finding out whom she can or cannot trust.

Our excerpt starts just after Corwin has refused to accept Denny's expensive sports car as a present, whereupon she has sent the vehicle hurtling over a cliff as if she were still inside it. Her emotional instability has one overall motivation not yet mentioned: the family have just been to a funeral; Denny's father is dead. Krantz, sitting in a car and spying on Denny, is a private investigator.

It is interesting to contrast Denny's mask of confidence, and the assurance and power she gains from her wealth, with the uncertainty, insecurity and naivety of some of the other young rebels in other plays represented in this book. Notice, too, the smooth technique, the assured professionalism of the scene.

Numbers in the margin are shot numbers as they appeared in the original script. Following them is a description of what the shot included. Several common production abbreviations are used:

   EXT - exterior
   INT - interior
   POV - point of view
   OS - off screen or off camera
   WIDE - wide angle shot

Commercial Break One

20   *EXT. BRICKWORKS DAY. POV from car as it moves past the office. We can see a man walking beside the building, look up as the car passes.*

21   POV NEW ANGLE. *Stop sign ignored. Passing through the intersection when a big truck brakes quickly.*

22   CAR AND TRUCK. *As Denny guns the motor and the car rushes on, towards the dirt road leading upwards. The man who was standing moves into frame to watch the car moving away.*

Truckdriver *(hollering from the truck).* Who the hell was that?

Man. That's your new boss. *(The truckdriver shakes his head in disgust and moves his truck.)*

23   EXT. CLAYPIT DAY. *The car moves too quickly up and around the circular dirt road leading to the high point of the spiral rise.*

24   TIGHT ON CAR. *Denny brings it to a stop and cuts the motor. The view is panoramic. Corwin sits quite still, not moving, buying back his breath. He turns to look over the ledge ahead of them.*

25   CORWIN'S POV. *The long way down to the bottom of the clay pit.*

26   CORWIN

Corwin *(turning angrily).* You need a good hard kick in the rump . . .

27   DENNY. *Smiling benignly.*

Corwin *(OS).* What do you think you're playing at?

28   DENNY AND CORWIN. *She slumps in her seat with a slight pout and he stares angrily, waiting for her answer.*

Corwin *(sarcastically).* Don't tell me I'm mistaken. That was your father they buried . . . *(She continues to pout.)* It wouldn't have killed you to get into the limousine like any normal bereaved daughter.

Denny *(looking up. Sharply).* Would that bring him back to life? *(That cools off and shuts up Corwin)* Why did you come, Greg?

Corwin *(tapping the car).* This.

Denny. It's yours.

Corwin *(shakes his head).* I don't want it.

Denny. I want you to have it.

Corwin. And I don't want it. I've got my own car. I've got my own clothes . . . cufflinks . . . watch . . . rings . . . Don't come on to me like I'm a gigolo.

29   DENNY STUNG

30   CORWIN SORRY

31   DENNY

Denny *(bitter reflectively)*. Wow, Doctor. You sure know how to draw blood. My father's still warm in his grave, I'm a brand new orphan . . . and the man I care the most about in all the world says he has to be paid to make love to me . . .

32 CORWIN

Corwin *(frustrated)*. I didn't say that. And stop playing hearts and flowers for me.

32 *DENNY. The sad face disappears and she pouts again.*

Corwin *(OS)*. What do I have to do to get through to you?

34 CORWIN AND DENNY. *He waits for an answer and she turns her face to him with its sexy little smile that says 'Do me'. Corwin turns away from her.*

Denny *(sexy pout)*. Greg. *(He refuses to face her or acknowledge.)* I haven't seen you for almost a month . . . *(runs her fingers up his arm)* Greg.

Corwin. Forget it.

Denny *(sits up angered by the rebuff)*. You don't want this car?

Corwin No.

Denny. Then get out. *(He looks at her now and sees the anger in her face. He nods and opening the door, gets out and slams it shut.)*

35 *DENNY. She looks up haughtily and starts up the motor.*

36 WIDE. *Corwin moves away, towards camera as Denny slowly backs the car towards camera. When she is abreast of him . . .*

Denny. It's still yours if you want it. *(Corwin says nothing and keeps walking.)*

37 *TIGHT ON FLOOR SHIFT. It is shifted into first.*

38 *TIGHT ON HAND THROTTLE. It is pulled out and the car roars to life.*

39 *TIGHT ON CORWIN. He hears the roar and turns quickly.*

40 *CORWIN'S POV. The car goes hurtling off the ledge.*

41 *TIGHT ON CORWIN. HORROR.*

Corwin *(screams)*. DENNY!!!

42 DENNY

Denny *(quietly)*. Yes.

43 *CORWIN. Wheels at the sound of the voice to find . . .*

44 *CORWIN AND DENNY. She is only a few feet from him.*

Corwin *(livid)*. You . . . Stupid little idiot . . . *(He moves quickly away from her.)*

Denny. It was my car. You said you didn't want it and I didn't need it . . . Awww. Come on, Greg. *(She starts after him and they both disappear from frame as we see in the distance that same Thunderbird. ZOOM towards it.)*

45   CORWIN AND DENNY *through a telephoto lens. Pan down to see the car in the pit, burning. Through this shot we can hear the whir of a movie camera.*

46   TIGHT ON KRANTZ. *He sits in his car and films what is happening and chuckles to himself because he gets such a great kick out of it. Krantz is about forty, distinguished-looking and immaculate.*

47   WIDE. DENNY AND CORWIN. *He is moving quickly and though she is running to catch up, her high heels cause her to lose ground.*

Denny *(shouting)*. I can't walk in these shoes, Greg. Don't leave me up here alone . . . Please Greg . . .

48   CORWIN DETERMINED AND ANGRY

49   DENNY FRUSTRATED BY THE HEELS

Denny *(shouting)*. Don't you know that I do these things because I love you. I want you to know I love you . . .

50   CORWIN IGNORING IT

Denny *(OS)*. Everytime you would have got into that car you would have thought about me . . . I want you to think about me . . .

51   DENNY. *She can't walk any faster or further. She stops.*

Denny *(shouting in pretended pain)*. Oh my ankle. *(She sits down.)*

52   CORWIN HEARS IT AND SHAKES HIS HEAD IN DISGUST

53   DENNY

Denny *(rubbing her foot and shouting)*. My ankle. I sprained it.

54   CORWIN

Denny *(OS)*. I really did, Greg. Don't leave me . . . *(Corwin stops and turns around.)*

55   CORWIN'S POV. *She sits on the dirt road, her shoes in her hand, still wearing her black veil.*

Denny. It really hurts.

56   CORWIN SOFTENING. *He walks back to her and drops to one knee to look at the ankle she's holding.*

Corwin. Where does it hurt? *(Pressing hard)* Here?

Denny *(hollering)*. Owww. That's it.

Corwin. You're a fake.

Denny. I am not a fake. It hurts right there where you pressed it. It's sprained I tell you. I know when I've sprained. something. If you were a doctor instead of a Psychiatrist, you'd know it was sprained. Now help me up and I'll limp along to a hospital . . .

Corwin. You've got to be the world's greatest living actress . . . *(Offers his hand.)*

Denny takes his hand and gets to her feet but she buckles on her 'sprained' ankle and he holds her close.

Corwin *(quietly. All anger gone)*. How do you propose we get you out of here?

Denny. I think you'll have to carry me.

Corwin *(nose to nose)*. I'll need to stop for frequent rests.

Denny *(seductively)*. I should hope so. *(They smile at each other and he lifts her into his arms.)*

57   DENNY AND CORWIN THROUGH LENS. *New angle from Krantz's POV as they move along the road.*

58   KRANTZ. *Dropping his camera from his eye. Shakes his head in envy. Sighs. Holds the lens over his palm to run out the tail of his film and opens the camera to change rolls. He opens the glove compartment of his car.*

59   GLOVE COMPARTMENT. *It is jammed with boxes of film. Krantz seems prepared for plenty of action.*

60   EXT. HIGHWAY. DAY. WIDE *as we see a cement truck moving out of traffic to enter the exit lane for downtown. As the truck passes we can see the lettering on the side of the cab 'ROBSON CEMENT'.*

61   INT. TRUCK CAB. DAY. TIGHT *on the driver, Art. He is about fifty with one of those leather faces in which all expression comes out of eye movements. He holds a stogie in his mouth and though his eyes are on the road, his ears are tuned in on the conversation. The shifting and blinking of his eyes tell us that Art thinks he is driving a couple of nuts.*

Denny *(OS)*. We could go out to the west coast . . .

WIDEN to include Corwin and Denny in the shot. She is in the centre and Corwin has his arm around her. Keep Art in foreground.

Denny. They've got all that oil on the beach at Santa Barbara . . .

62   CORWIN AND DENNY

Denny *(snuggling to him).* Wouldn't it be great to strip down and roll in that oily goo?

63 ART. HIS EYES ROLL

Corwin *(OS).* You roll in the oily goo.

64 DENNY AND CORWIN

Corwin. I've got to earn some money.

Denny *(pouting).* Money. Money. Money. That's all you ever talk about.

Corwin. I can't afford to drive six thousand cars over cliffs . . .

65 ART. LISTENING

Denny *(OS).* Five thousand . . . See, you don't even know the value of money. You would have paid six.

66 CORWIN AND DENNY

Corwin. I know that Doctor James is paying two hundred and fifty a week and that's five times what I earn in the hospital . . .

Denny *(sitting up in a pout).* I'm sorry I ever told you about Doc James. We could have spent two nice weeks together.

Corwin. I'm not much for rolling in oily goo . . .

Denny. I think you'd be great, Doctor . . .

67 ART. LISTENING

Denny *(OS).* If you'd stop looking for all those Freudian symbols.

68 DENNY AND CORWIN

Denny. It gives you too many hang ups . . . *(Corwin smiles at her turn-about psychoanalysis. She turns to Art.)*

69 CORWIN DENNY AND ART

Denny. Come on, Arthur, Open her up. Let's see what she's got . . .

70 TIGHT ON ACCELERATOR. *Art's foot presses lightly on the accelerator. Denny's shoeless foot comes over and presses down on his foot.*

Denny *(OS).* Let's go. This is no funeral. . . .

71 EXT. DOWNTOWN EXPRESSWAY. DAY. *The truck approaching and zooming past.*

72 EXT. ROBSON HOUSE. DAY. WIDE. *The house is a large mansion. There is a Cadillac in the driveway. The cement truck enters frame and stops at the curb.*

73 INT. TRUCK CAB. DAY. CORWIN, DENNY AND ART

Corwin *(looking out the window at the house).* That's quite a bungalow.

Denny. Drop around tonight and I'll give you the grand tour . . . *(to Art)* Thank you Arthur for an excitingly breathtaking ride . . . *(chucking him under the chin)* And don't you worry about the speeding ticket. I'll take care of it. *(Art is glum as Corwin opens the door and gets out.)*

74 EXT. CEMENT TRUCK. DAY. CORWIN AND DENNY. *Corwin is out and helps Denny to the sidewalk. He holds her in his embrace longer than necessary and there is a quiet moment when the defenses are down between them and they look into each other's eyes . . .*

Denny *(softly).* Don't be a stranger. *(He smiles at the redundancy of the statement and lets her go.)*

Corwin. I'll try and see you tonight. *(She smiles and starts walking away as he swings up into the cab.)* Hey. *(She turns.)* What happened to your sprained ankle?

75 DENNY. *Realizes her faux pas and shrugs. She turns back to her walk but this time she limps dramatically.*

76 INT. TRUCK CAB. DAY. ART AND CORWIN. *Art is in foreground as Corwin swings himself into the cab and slams the door.*

Corwin *(to Art).* Next stop. The Psychiatric Hospital.

Art. You ain't kidding. *(He throws the truck in gear and pulls away.)*

HOLD *shot as truck pulls out of frame and we are left with a shot of Denny walking with her exaggerated limp, up the walk to the house. She turns at the sound of the truck leaving and loses her limp.*

77 DENNY. NEW ANGLE *as she moves around Caddy in the driveway and up the steps. She stops at the door.*

78 TIGHT ON DENNY. *She hesitates at the door. The impish, fun-girl has vanished and we see a trace of fear in her eyes as she looks at the great door. With a forced resolve, she opens the door to enter.*

79 INT. ROBSON HOUSE FOYER. DAY. DENNY *as she comes through the door and closes it behind her. She leans her back on it for a moment and then moves forward.* MOVING *with her as she reaches the doorway to the living room which is open. We can see Evelyn and Carol seated in the room while the butler, Carson, is extending a tray with tea and cake. Denny moves quickly into the room.*

80 INT. LIVING ROOM. DAY. WIDE. *Evelyn and Carol look up as Denny approaches.*

Evelyn *(admonishing tone).* Where have you been?

Denny *(slumping into a chair in a very unlady-like pose).* Living and loving.

(Carol hides a small smile for her mother's bruised modesty. Evelyn looks in horror and distaste at her niece. Denny's black dress looks wrinkled and mud-stained. Her legs and ankles reveal mud and grass stains.)

Denny *(ignoring her aunt as she turns her attention to Carson).* How are you Carson?

Carson *(stiffly and with a touch of fear).* I'm fine thank you, Miss Denny. Please accept my deepest sympathies for your tragic loss . . .

81 *DENNY*

Denny *(smiles benignly).* And please accept my sympathies for *your* tragic loss.

82 *CARSON. QUIZZICALLY*

83 *DENNY*

Denny. You're fired.

84 *GROUP. Evelyn looks shocked. Carson is stunned.*

Evelyn. You can't mean that . . .

Denny. Why can't I? It's my house. *(to Carson)* And tell the housekeeper and the cook. They're fired too. I want you all out of here before dinner. You'll get one month's severance pay and a glowing letter of recommendation from me.

Evelyn. These people have been with your father for an entire generation.

Denny *(interrupting).* Yes, Aunt Evelyn. And this house has been in the family for five generations. And I'm still selling it.

85 *EVELYN*

Evelyn. You can't do that.

86 *DENNY*

Denny *(snapping her fingers).* Just like *that*.

Hunting Stuart

Robertson Davies

First published 1972
First production Toronto, 1955, by Crest Theatre

From Act II
Characters in the excerpt: Stuart, Lilian, Carol, Fred, Clemmie, Dr. Shrubsole, Dr. Sobieska, Telephone voice of Mrs. Orville Gilkinson

This play was written in 1955 for the Crest Theatre Company led by Donald Davis and Barbara Chilcott, who played Stuart and Dr. Sobieska respectively. It has all the genial humour and gentle irony we expect of Robertson Davies. Henry Benedict Stuart is a minor civil servant, handsome, modest in his expectations, and seemingly contented with his undistinguished life. His wife, Lilian, is a social climber in a small way, proud of her postmaster father and her remote connections with English gentry. She is much embarrassed by her husband's lack of ambition and his aunt Clemmie's local notoriety as a testifier in advertisements to the efficacy of various products and patent medicines. Carol, the Stuarts' young daughter is in love with Fred, a stolid psychology student.

This middle-class family situation is suddenly disrupted by the arrival of two inquirers into problems of heredity, Dr. Homer Shrubsole and Dr. Maria Sobieska, who are convinced that they can prove Mr. Stuart to be a direct descendent of Bonnie Prince Charlie, thus making him Pretender to the English throne. With the aid of a curious powder, administered like snuff, the doctors demonstrate Stuart's royal heritage by causing him to relive a portion of a previous life he led as Bonny Prince Charlie. Heredity, it turns out, hands down to us memories of our ancestors' existence. The powder merely helps to release the memories. Stuart's discovery of his hidden greatness brings Canadian middle-class life into headlong collision with the disturbing selfishness, zest and extravagance of flamboyant nobility from a far less inhibited age than ours. Stuart, at the end of the play, faces a choice between the pursuit of his newly found greatness and the resumption of humdrum normality.

In our excerpt, we witness some of the experimenting with the powder, in which Stuart becomes every inch a prince, albeit in exile. He mistakes his wife, Lilian, for Prince Charlie's mistress, Walkinshaw, and thinks that Elsie Gilkinson of a local women's organization is nothing but an upstart dwarf. The contrast between the grand airs of Stuart the Prince and his ordinary family is matched by the contrast between the fine old Victorian mansion in Ottawa, the top floor of which is the Stuart apartment, and the tawdry, pretentious way in which it is furnished. Back right is a kitchen area with a counter top separating it from the dining area front right. The rest of the stage is the living room.

The scene is the principal room in the apartment of Henry Benedict Stuart, a minor civil servant, in Ottawa, Canada. Our first impression is one of clutter and fussiness of a rather pathetic sort; so much has been done, and done so badly, to make this room home-like and fashionable in the convention of the ladies' magazines. But the room itself resists both the striving toward fashion and the trend toward vulgarity. It is the biggest room on the top floor of an old Victorian mansion; the walls bend inward, following the contours of the roof; there are large windows, curious in shape and too near the floor. It is an undefeated old monster of a room.

It serves the purpose of three rooms. At the rear, on the right of an actor facing the audience, a 'kitchen-area' has been devised by means of a half-partition with a counter top, dividing it from the rest of the room; in front of this pathetic bit of pretence is the 'dining-area', which has a table and chairs of a cheap and pretentious kind. The rest is the 'living-area', and though it may be littered with little pots of ivy, little ashtrays, little tables with little boxes on them and little trash of every description, there is a decent old sofa, and a bearable chair or two. The door from downstairs is at the actor's right; the door into the rest of the flat is up a few steps and off a platform with a baluster, left.

Here is a challenge, then, for the scene designer. Let him give us a room in which the good old quality of the house is swearing at the cheap decorations of its present occupants. Let him give us a setting which is capable of being hideous, pathetic, and, when occasion demands, noble. When he has read the play he will find out why.

Stuart. I hate whispers! *(His eyes flash open for the first time.)* Though it is my fate to sojourn here with a pack of Scotchmen, Poles, Italians and brandy-nipping English whores I shall at least be treated as a gentleman, if not as a king. Let me hear no more whispering! God's my life, I must have sleep in my eyes, you look so queer! Walkinshaw! Where are you? *(He advances upon Lilian.)* What are you skulking there for, heh? Get me something to drink, my charmer, and be quick about it.

Lilian. What—what would you like—Sire?

Stuart. What would I like? *Nom de Dieu,* what question's that? What do I always like? What would I like? Walkinshaw, the brandy has washed your small brain away!

Lilian. What should I give him?

Shrubsole. What have you got?

Clemmie. Here's my payday bottle, not even opened. Ben always loved a drop o'Scotch. Try it.

Lilian. Why does he call me Walkinshaw?

Shrubsole. She was the Pretender's most faithful friend till death. She was also his mistress.

Lilian *(greatly pleased).* His mistress? Well, that's not how I would ever have thought of myself. Still, it shows that it's not so ridiculous to suppose I might have appealed to Prince Charlie as you thought. *(Pours out a very small drink in a tumbler.)* What shall we put with this? I haven't a drop of soda in the house.

Carol. There's a Coke in the fridge.

Lilian. Does that seem right to you? Scotch and Coke for Bonnie Prince Charlie?

Shrubsole. If it's the best you have.

Dr. Sobieska. It sounds disgusting.

Stuart. Walkinshaw, I'm waiting!

Lilian. Here is your drink, Sire.

Stuart *(drinking). Mort de ma vie,* it's poison! The Presbyterians are trying to poison me! *(He spews it out.)* Walkinshaw, have you turned against me?

Lilian. Me? How could you think so? 'Ower Leal—Ower Leal!'

Stuart. 'Ower' what? What's the matter with you, Walkinshaw?

Lilian. Surely the king of the Highland hearts recognises the old old Highland tongue? 'More than loyal', Sire.

Stuart. I haven't been king of the Highland hearts, or of anything else, for some time, you old fool, and well you should know it. What have you to do with any tongue but the English tongue, you London slut? And don't prate to me of your loyalty; those who parade their loyalty hope to gain by it. Now—what's this filth?

Lilian. Whisky.

Stuart. Ye lie. It's a vile wine, made from turnips and horse-piss. Why would you offer me whisky? You know I hate it.

Lilian. It's all we have, Sire.

Stuart. O Poverty, thy tooth is keen! No wine? Only the raw usquebaugh of the bare-breached North? Well, get me the bottle. Fish, I've lodged in some lousy cribs in my time, but none worse than this. *(Lilian has brought him the whisky bottle.)* Now, Walkinshaw, you old blackleg, we'll make a night of it. Get the cards.

Lilian. We haven't any cards.

Stuart. Get the cards, woman.

Dr. Sobieska *(producing cards)* Here is a little patience deck. Use these.

Carol. He doesn't know how to play cards.

Shrubsole. Wonderful! Now, Mr. Lewis, what have you to say about inherited memory?

Stuart. What money have you, Walkinshaw? I haven't a sou.

Lilian. Just my housekeeping money, Sire.

Stuart. Give it to me. Now—win it back if you can. You deal. And roll up your sleeves. I know you, madam.

Lilian, much discomposed, begins to deal as for bridge. He eyes her sardonically, then suddenly dashes the cards to the floor.

Are you possessed, woman? What do I want with ten cards? Pick them up and deal again.

Lilian. I will not.

Stuart. How's this? Do you brave me, Walkinshaw? Have you forgotten the weight of my stick, bitch? Pick up the cards!

Shrubsole. You'd better, I think.

Dr. Sobieska. It is on record that he once gave Walkinshaw fifty beatings in one day.

Lilian *(picking up the cards, tearfully)* I only meant that a gentleman would pick them up himself, when he threw them down.

Stuart *(softening).* Yes, wench, a gentleman might, but would a king do it for a subject? And are you not all my subjects, dearest heart? Is not my whole earthly kingdom locked up in your breast, my faithful Tatty? You must bear with my fancies, dear girl, as I must bear with the world's disorder that makes me the wretched pensioner of the man who sits on my throne. Let's drink to German Geordie! *(He pulls her onto his lap, and lifts the bottle to her lips; she drinks a little, with difficulty.)* What's the matter, mouse? Are you longing for your brandy? *(Takes the bottle and has a long pull at it.)*

Lilian. Stop! You'll be ill in the morning.

Stuart. I've been ill every morning for twenty years. *(Drinks again.)* When I was running for my life in '45, I drank this tipple by the hornful in every croft in the Western Isles; for seven months I was never dry or sober. Seven months: that's long enough to make a poor sort of child, Tatty, and it was long enough to make a poor sort of creature out of me. But still I am a king, lass, though a king with but one subject; and that one subject, my sweetest mouse, is worth all the world together.

He has finished the bottle and is now very drunk, but he holds it well, speaks with more than normal clarity, and staggers only a little. The drunkenness is in his wild and rolling eye, and in his raffish smile.

I'll walk abroad now. Put on your bonnet, Walkinshaw, and we'll show ourselves in the fashionable part of the city. With luck we may meet some fools who do not play picquet as well as we do.

Lilian. No, no; you mustn't go out!

Stuart. I will go out. *(He shies the bottle at her head.)*

Lilian. No—see, we have guests. You cannot leave them.

Stuart. I can leave if I choose. What guests? Who's that?

Shrubsole *(bowing).* I am a physician, Chevalier.

Stuart. A chirurgeon? Have you come to give me a purge? Your face is purge enough, you dog. Get out.

Shrubsole. I am a royal physician, Sire. Attending here upon the Princess Maria Clementina Sobieska.

Dr. Sobieska curtsies deeply.

Stuart. My mother was a Sobieska. Are you a cousin of mine?

Dr. Sobieska. I have that honour, Sire.

Stuart *(all charm now).* I am truly sorry, cousin, to entertain you in so poor a place. *(For the first time, he is conscious of the whole room.)* Come here, child, and kiss your cousin. My daughter, the Duchess d'Albany. *(Carol is confused.)* My old nurse, also a Sobieska. *(Clemmie, ready for anything, curtsies profoundly.)* Of Mistress Walkinshaw you will have heard from the tongue of scandal; an honest trollop, except at cards, and she has shared my exile without much complaint. *(to Fred)* Boy, bring wine.

Fred. There isn't any wine.

Stuart *(silky).* What is that bottle I see there? *(It is the other whisky bottle.)*

Fred. It's whisky.

Stuart. Bring it.

Sulkily, Fred does so, assisted by Carol, who brings tumblers.

> Pour, Walkinshaw. Cousin, let us drink to better fortune. I am sorry there is no wine. *(Holds up a glass of whisky.)* This we must look upon as a Pretender—the second in the room. Boy, have we nothing to eat?

Fred. How should I know?

Stuart. The insolence of Italian servants would be intolerable if it were not amusing. I shall prepare food. I am an excellent cook. I have to be. Walkinshaw is English; she spoils everything. I shall prepare an omelet. *(He goes into the kitchen area, and is soon breaking eggs into a bowl.)*

Carol. But he can't cook anything.

Shrubsole. This is beyond my wildest hope. Poppet, we've done it!

Dr. Sobieska. Bibi, it's a dream come true. And isn't it wonderful?

Lilian. No. I'm frightened. Why am I Walkinshaw? Didn't he have a wife?

Shrubsole. He had Walkinshaw much longer.

Carol. He called me Duchess—something.

Dr. Sobieska. Duchess d'Albany; his daughter. He was very fond of her.

Carol. But I don't want to be a Duchess. I hate all this! It's spooky and dishonest and—and wrong. This is Canada. This is now!

Dr. Sobieska. We've no time for that. Perhaps 'now' is a little bigger than you suspect. Perhaps you are somewhat better bred than anyone could guess.

Fred. Don't take that tone with Carol, Doctor Whatever-it-is. I'm going to call the police. You two ought to be locked up.

Shrubsole. Please, Mr. Harris, control yourself. Because this is beyond you—

Fred. You're troublemakers. I'm going to ring the police now.

At which moment the telephone rings, and, as Fred is beside it, he answers.

Yes? Just a minute. Mrs. Stuart, it's for you.

But Lilian is staring before her, and does not hear.

Dr. Sobieska. Walkinshaw! You are wanted on the telephone.

Lilian. Hello?

In a daze, she takes the instrument from Fred.

Phone Voice. Lilian Stuart, where are you?

Lilian. Hello, who is that?

Phone Voice. Lil, you know perfectly well who it is. It's Elsie. Elsie Gilkinson. The girls are all sitting here, waiting for you to give your paper.

Lilian. Paper?

Phone Voice. Lil, are you sick? Your paper on 'Some Canadian Pioneer Families Connected with the Nobility and Gentry of Great Britain'. Do you mean to say you've forgotten? Lil, there are two hundred and fifty of the girls here, and they've waited half an hour—

Lilian is transfixed by the telephone, trying to sort out her worlds. Stuart has come in with his bowl of broken eggs; we have seen him, during the preparation of this dish, finish the second bottle of whisky and fling it on the floor. He goes to Lilian.

Stuart. Walkinshaw, whisk the eggs! What the plague is that thing? Am I mad, or do I hear a hobgoblin's squeak coming from it? Give it to me! *(He thrusts the bowl upon Lilian and listens to the telephone in wonder.)* Is it a toy? *(As he speaks, we hear faintly the voice of Elsie Gilkinson: 'I really think, Lil, that after all your years in the club you'd be the last to forget our regular fortnightly meeting. I guess I don't need to tell you that a lot of the girls associate your failure to appear tonight with that picture of Mrs. Izzard that was in The Journal tonight. The Journal* and *The Citizen. Now Lil, this isn't a time for false pride; if you expect to get on the National*

Executive—and I know you do—that picture isn't going to make it any easier, but you'll lose out for sure if you show the white feather now. . . . ' etc.) By God it's a dwarf! A dwarf in a box! Ahoy there! Dwarfie, can ye sing? Sing 'When the King Enjoys His Own Again'!

Phone Voice. Who's that? Lil, who's that shouting? Who are you?

Stuart. Dwarf, I am Charles Edward Louis Philip Casimir. Who are you?

Phone Voice. This is Mrs. Orville Gilkinson, Regent of the Clara Faucett McGurk Chapter of—

Stuart *(fending off the distracted Lilian, and shouting).* He says he's a Regent! The dwarf says he's a Regent! Curse o' God, I'll have your guts for garters! *(He flings the instrument down, and it is heard squawking with dismay.)* Walkinshaw, I leave the omelet to you. Don't burn it.

Lilian. Oh, I'm ruined. Utterly, utterly runied!

Burlap Bags

Len Peterson

Published 1972
First broadcast 1946, by C.B.C. Radio

From Act 1
Characters in the excerpt: Manitoba, Finley, Tannahill, Shapes A,B,C,D,E, Busy People, Fun-Lovers

Len Peterson was born in 1917 in Regina, where he attended Luther College before going to Northwestern University. He served in the army during World War II. He has travelled widely, has written articles, stories, a novel, *Chipmunk* (1949), and has adapted many works for radio and television, besides writing an enormous number of original works for these two media. His stage play about Eskimo life, *The Great Hunger* (1960), has been highly praised. In all, he has written over a thousand works for radio, television, film and stage.

Burlap Bags (1946) is probably the most important historically of his radio plays because it anticipates by several years the experimental plays of Samuel Becket and Eugene Ionesco. Peterson presents two down and outs, Finley and Manitoba, in a shoddy rooming house. Manitoba, hearing of the suicide of Tannahill, a lonely, withdrawn man, has been to the funeral and returned with a pair of rubber overshoes and a manuscript journal he has taken from the dead man's room. Within this realistic situation, a phantasmagoria develops in which Tannahill is shown as a man who sees clearly, as he thinks, whereas other people wear burlap bags over their heads. They are thus insulated within their illusions. When Tannahill eventually succumbs to the temptation to wear a burlap bag, he finds that there are none left.

Our excerpt comes from the beginning of this one act play. It is taken not from the original radio script, but from the revised version for the stage, since this has been published and is therefore readily available. The scene is a sordid room, but by a transition made possible by lighting changes, this reality gives way to the non-realistic fantasy of the middle part of the play. In the radio script, these transitions were achieved through musical and sound effects. The same could be done in combination with lighting if so desired in a stage presentation. Notice also that a sharp contrast in acting styles is demanded by the change from the realistic opening to the scenes in Limbo.

Today. A room in a rooming house, transformed for awhile to limbo. Manitoba of the Lower Strata is enjoying a hunk of bread and a piece of summer sausage by himself. It is almost a love affair. But a knock on the door interrupts him.

Finley *(outside).* Manitoba! Manitoba!

Manitoba tries to down what is left of the bread and sausage while the pounding continues.

Manitoba!

The door begins to open. Manitoba rushes over to hold it shut, but the visitor Finley is too strong, so Manitoba capitulates and greets him warmly.

Manitoba. Finley! I was hoping you'd turn up—and share this with me.

Breaking the bread and sausage, he offers the smaller portions to his friend Finley, who comes from the same social set.

Finley. Where was you this afternoon? I was around to see you; my place is so cold! I come up here to your room, and you—

Manitoba. I was at a funeral.

Finley. A what?

Manitoba. A funeral.

Finley. Who died?

Manitoba. Some guy up on the third floor of this rooming house. Had a service at the Gospel Hall.

Finley. What he die of?

Manitoba. Gas. Crazy fool! Did it in the night. Turned on the gas. We mighta all been killed.

Finley. Why he do it?

Manitoba. I d'know. He was a bit nuts, never spoke. And wore glasses half-inch thick. And you shoulda seen his room, Finley, full of medicine bottles.

Finley. Was he sick?

Manitoba. If he wunt naturally, all that medicine musta made him sick sure. You know that rubby down the hall, Smitty?

Finley. Yeah.

Manitoba. He drank all the stuff smelled like alcohol. 'At was last night. Still lying on his bed groaning. Everybody in the house went up to the guy's room and took something. He didn't have no relatives. I wasn't going to take nothing, but when I saw everybody else going up—and if we didn't take it, the cops woulda.

Finley. What you get?

Manitoba. All those hogs took everything! All that was left when I got there was a pair of rubbers. The old guy always wore rubbers—only he wunt so old, less'n forty.

Finley. Huh, good rubbers, nice thick soles.

Manitoba. Yeah, but they're too big for me. They oughta fit you, eh? *(kicking them toward his friend)* Try'm on, Finley.

Finley. They look my size.

Manitoba. Sell'm to you.

Finley *(grunting as he stoops over).* Yeah, fit. Just right.

Manitoba. Sell'm to you. Half a buck.

Finley. No good to you. Why'n't you give them to me? Didn't cost you nothing, Manitoba.

Manitoba. What you mean? Wasted a whole afternoon at the guy's funeral. Why shouldn't I get half a buck outa him?—Okay, thirty-five cents. Coulda made more'n that bumming this afternoon. Mighta evena found me a job. Come on, you got the money! Look at the thick soles.

Finley. Ain't I ever give you anything?

Manitoba. So I don't get nothing outa the guy? Mrs. Salichuck got his watch, and Samuels got a couple of good shirts, and his coat, and Branscher got his glasses —he looked funny in his coffin without his glasses, and Evans got an armful of books he's already sold to the bookstore down the street, and I don't know what the Focklers got, but it was plenty! Smitty did all right too with the medicine, even if he got sick. But all I got was a pair of rubbers that I can't get thirty-five cents for!

Finley. You was stupid, that's all. Why'n't you beat the others to it?

Manitoba. Because I happen to have a bit of respect for the dead, which the others ain't got, 'at's why! The place was stripped bare when I got there. All 'at was left was them medicine bottles, and some papers on the dresser *(producing them),* and the rubbers. How they missed them rubbers, you got me. I brought the papers down too, and read them. *(handing them to Finley)* The guy was screwy in the head all right. He wrote it, see, there's his name, Tannahill. Go on, read it while I sew up my pants. *(showing a hole in the front of his trousers)* Ripped them on a nail that was sticking out of the goof's coffin. I never read such stuff. *(producing a needle and thread)* Ask me: the guy shoulda been locked up.

Finley. It's neat writing though, Manitoba.

Manitoba. Yeah, but wait'll you read it.

Finley *(reading).* "There was nothing to be seen at first.

As he reads the stage darkens.

There was only blackness and voices. The voices I heard only when I was alone at night, and lay face-down on my bed . . .

Burlap Bags

Blackness. Out of the blackness come short-lived patches of dim light and simple, eerie Voices that slowly become amorphous Shapes moving about.

A. It' awfully dark in here. Why doesn't somebody put the lights on? Where's the light switch?

B. There isn't any light switch.

A. Why isn't there? Then somebody light a match.

C. Mine are all wet. I've been sucking them. But I guess they're not phosphorous. I don't feel sick at all.

A. There must be a light switch somewhere—or at least a candle in this room.

C. We're not in a room.

B. Yes, we are.

C. No, we're outside, walking down a street.

D. We're in a piano box. But it's lucky the piano's been taken out. Be rather crowded otherwise.

C. If this's a piano box why don't we bump into the sides?

D. Because it moves with us.

A. You're logical.

D. Yes, I know.

E. I'm looking for my wife. Has anybody seen her?

B. What does she look like?

E. I've forgotten.

B. Don't be silly, how could you forget?

E. It's very simple.

D. You're lucky.

A. Let's go sideways for while.

C. No, let's go in every direction.

A. At the same time?

C. Of course, you fool!

D. Oh, that should be interesting. Yes, let's!

A light comes up on one upright figure, Tannahill, a rootless man, wearing thick glasses. The amorphous Shapes continue to flow around him.

Tannahill. I knew what it was. It was disillusionment. I had had the usual beliefs and hopes. I don't know when it happened. I've lost track of time. I can't sort out the time at all. The beliefs went all out of shape, and the hopes vanished. As I remember it was very painful. Everyone else kept on being motivated by those same beliefs and hopes. It seemed absurd. I have an impression of myself standing still, somewhere in space, watching the world drift away. And I said to myself many times, "All is nonsense." Those crazy creatures in the dark were as sensible as any . . .

C. That's a very interesting book you're reading. Are you enjoying it?

D. Oh, yes, very much.

C. That's certainly the best way to read it, with your eyes shut.

D. I read for knowledge as well as amusement.

C. I imagined you did.

D. I find that I learn more by reading this book at fifty paces—and upside down —and closed.

C. What's the name of it, if you don't mind my asking?

D. The same as the movie. Here, smell it. It's a best seller, before it's published.

A. Let's dance.

E. Greco-Roman or catch-as-catch-can?

A. Greco-Roman.

The Shapes flow away and disappear. But immediately there are new manifestations around Tannahill, sober-minded, busy People moving around with the accoutrements of commerce.

Tannahill. I found it difficult to work. Why work? To what end? I still went to the office and checked ledgers, and consulted files, and wrote inter-office memos, and sent out letters teeming with flattery and clichés. It was all a devil's joke, and nobody knew it but me.

He turns from the Busy People to yet other manifestations, to the Fun-Lovers with their accoutrements.

Tannahill. What was worse, I found it difficult to play and enjoy myself. No matter what the fun, someone in the middle of it would have to stop and run back to work for awhile. The rules of the game got all mixed up with the rules of business that way, and it stopped being a game for fun and became a game for keeps. The diamonds became real diamonds, the clubs real clubs, and the spades real spades.

He flees the Fun-Lovers and the Busy People, who have now become indistinguishable.

With a hi money money, and you'll be the life of the party, my son, if you've got the bank etchings.

And he lies down.

How good it was to go to bed, and pull the blankets over my head, and stay that way, and shut out the world.

Some of the amorphous Shapes flow around him again as the lights fade almost to blackness.

Marsh Hay

Merrill Denison

Published 1923

From Act II
Characters in the excerpt: Walt, Thompson, Tom, Nosse, Barnood, John, Three Youths

    Merrill Denison was born in Detroit, Michigan in 1893. He studied at the universities of Toronto, Pennsylvania and Paris. He served in the First World War and later became director of Hart House Theatre, Toronto. During this period he began writing plays which enjoyed great popularity for decades.
    The marsh hay in the play represented here is the essence of life and labour in the Northern backwoods community in which the action takes place. It is a kind of trap, involving work and marriage and facing the consequences of one's actions—at least, so it seems to the rebellious young Walt, who is trying to wriggle out of a paternity suit. "I ain't," he declares, "goin' to stick in the backcountry all my life, cuttin' marsh hay and raisin' kids. No, I won't marry no one." Walt is a forerunner of the problem youngsters of the television and film dramas of the 'sixties. But, whereas they become aware of their own problems and of the defects of society at large, Walt's rebellion is simpler, a matter of selfishness and instinct, the struggle of a raw youth to evade punishment.
    Our excerpt captures some of the local setting as well as a quality of life which Denison neatly conveys through the dialogue and the attitudes and naiveties of the characters. It also presents the comic reversal of Walt making a swaggering, self-confident entry which quickly changes at Thompson's intervention to a running exit in pursuit of his would-be father-in-law. The scene demands that everyone involved react to the situation all the time, for detailed attention to stage business will help to establish personality, particularly in the case of the mean-souled Nosse.

The interior of a general store. A long counter occupies the rear of the store and behind it are shelves with bolts of cloth on them. At one end of the counter is the post office wicket, next to it an open space for the serving of customers, scales and a show case. Harness, shanty boots, pans, the tools of human existence in the north country, hang in cluttered strings from the ceiling. The entrance from the street is at the left, that into the house at the right. Beyond the street door is a large window. The space in front of the counter is taken up by a large box stove and scattered around it are up-ended boxes, which serve as seats.

Tad Nosse, the storekeeper, a small, fair man with drooping moustaches, is leaning over the counter talking to William Thompson, an elderly man with the city stamp upon him. A prospector, horse trader, a lawyer, an amateur backwoodsman, whom ambition and economic necessity forced to the city.

Nosse. Harye, Walt. Didn't send you down, eh? Come on in and tell us all about it and have a cigar. Where's the rest of them? Where's Black John? What happened?

Walt Roche comes in the door in the middle of Nosse's speech. There is nothing of the villain about him. He is a light, good looking lad of medium height and carries himself with a distinct swagger. He is followed by his brother Tom. Three other youths, the ever present tail to any kite of excitement, drift in after them. Walt is very sure of himself for he goes directly to Thompson, with whom he shakes hands.

Walt. Harye, Mr. Thompson? Back again for a hunt?

Thompson. Hello, Walt. How are the deer this year? Lots of them, eh? Hello, Tom. How's everything with you? Hear you've been married since I was back last. How do you like it?

Tom *(a rather shy chap)*. It aint too bad. I got me a good woman. Tessie Serang.

Nosse. Have a cigar, Walt?

Walt. I don't mind if I do.

He saunters over to the show case and takes the cigar offered to him by Nosse, who even goes to the extent of lighting it for him.

Nosse. Tom?

Tom shakes his head and Nosse hurriedly puts the box away as one of the other boys steps up. The three unnamed boys distribute themselves on boxes while Walt takes the centre of the stage before the stove, very much in the limelight.

Walt *(critically)*. It aint a bad cigar.

Nosse *(impatiently)*. Old man Spenton let you off, eh? Was it old man Spenton tried you? *(Walt bides his time.)*

Tom. Yes, it was Spenton.

Barnood *(to Thompson)*. Old man Spenton, down to Hendale.

Thompson. That isn't the old chap that used to keep the hotel across from the Methodist Church?

Nosse. That's him. Give it up when they took away the bars.

Thompson. But I thought he was only a justice of the peace.

Barnood. That's all old Sam is.

Walt. He's a good man, old Sam. He seen right away he couldn't hold me for nothin. Oncet I told him how it was and told him there was four other lads willin to swear I wasn't the only one he seen he couldn't hold me. Old John was rarin mad but it didn't do him no good.

Barnood *(severely).* It seems to me you was pretty lucky to get off. Not only you, but the whole pack of you, if what you say is true.

Nosse. Was there many down to it?

Tom. It was pretty well packed till old Sam sent everybody out but Walt and John and some witnesses.

Thompson. Wasn't the girl there?

Walt. Sarilin? Her maw wouldn't let her come, would she, Tom? *(Tom shakes his head.)* It was this way . . .

Thompson. This is a strange business, Andy. The most material witness not present and the case tried before a justice of the peace. The thing's absurd.

Walt. Nothin strange about it that I can see. First of all when we went in Sam ast Black John to tell what he had to say and he says how Sarilin said I was the one got her into trouble.

Nosse. What did you say?

Walt. I spoke right up, didn't I Tom? And I says, if she says that, she's lyin and I can prove she's lyin. She don't know who done it and she can't prove who done it. Sam asts me what I meant and the lads there *(pointing to the three boys)* says they was willin to swear. Didn't you? *(The three nod their heads.)*

One of them. Sure, I'm willin to swear.

Another. Me, too.

Walt. You see. He couldn't find nothin agin me. I says so before they had me arrested.

Thompson. Did Spenton dismiss the case entirely?

Walt. He says the only thing for John to do was to try and settle in a friendly sort of way between ourselves and if we couldn't he says somethun about a trial at Belleville or somewheres if John wanted to go on with it. But I aint afraid of goin to Belleville or anywheres else.

Barnood. Told you to settle it out of court, did he? are you going to do the right thing and marry her?

Walt *(indignantly).* No. What the hell would I want to be tied to her for the rest of my life for? I aint goin to stick in the backcountry all my life, cuttin marsh hay and raisin kids. No, I won't marry no one.

Thompson. You should pay her doctor's bills anyway. That's the least you can do, Walt.

Walt. I aint goin to pay a cent, Mr. Thompson. Why should I? Her old woman's gettin more fun out'n this'n she ever got in her life before. Aint you heard how they're all actin? Wont let Sarilin raise her hand to do a thing. They wait on her like they was slaves.

Barnood. It's my opinion that John'll make you pay.

Walt. How'll he make me? *(Unseen by everyone but Thompson and Barnood, John Serang comes in the door.)* He wouldn't've had me arrested even if it hadn't been for his old woman. She made him do it. He was afraid to do anythin to me. He's afraid of paw. *(John has walked to a position immediately behind Walt and has been seen by everyone except the boy. With the exception of the two older men, Thompson and Barnood, all cringe away from him. His hand is above Walt's shoulder. Walt goes on talking.)* He's been afraid of paw ever since they shantied together on the Mipin . . .

John *(his hand closing on Walt's shoulder).* Afraid of your paw?

Walt *(thoroughly frightened).* Let me go. Damn it, let me go. Let me go, I tell you.

John. Afraid of your paw? Bah! I licked him at Cemetery Shoots and I licked him at Ragged Rapids.

Walt. Let me go.

John. Afraid? I'll lick him to-day, too.

Barnood. Let the youngster go, John. You'll do no good thay way. Come over here and sit down.

Serang lets Walt go and comes over to where Barnood and Thompson are.

John. Is that you, Lawyer Thompson?

Thompson. Hello, John. Been having quite a time of it, eh?

John. Been doin some teamin. Had to pay all the bills that's comin in.

Barnood. Look here, John. Why don't you two settle this thing between yourselves right here? The lads say that's what Spenton told you. Settle it between yourselves.

John *(menacingly, taking a step forward).* I'm willing to settle it.

Barnood. How about you, Walt? Will you listen to reason?

Walt *(considering the chances of escape).* Sure I'll listen. Though there aint nothin to listen to.

Thompson. You ought to do something, that's certain. John, what is the least you'll take to drop the whole business?

John. By rights, he ought to marry her. She's his now.

Walt. She aint neither. And I aint going to marry her. What'd I marry her for? Settle down like you and try to scrape a living off'n your place?

John. I'll make you . . .

Thompson. You can't make him marry her, John. You might in some communities. The people might make it too hot for him.

Barnood. There's no chancet of that back here, now. Not with the way John's woman has been actin and the way she treated the minister.

John. Well, he ought to pay the doctor's bills anyways and pay me somethun a week while I got to feed 'em.

Barnood. Suppose he gave you a couple of hundred dollars?

Walt. Where'd I get a couple of hundred dollars?

John. You'll have to pay somethun.

Walt. I wont pay a damn cent. I don't have to and I wont. And you daren't touch me, neither.

Barnood places himself between Walt and John. The others rise, expecting a fight.

John. By God, I'll make you. I'll make you pay every bill there is.

Walt. How'll you make me? By havin the law on me? You done that oncet and you aint got much out'n it.

John. I'll find a way of makin you . . .

Thompson, to avoid the fight which seems inevitable, takes John by the arm and leads him toward the front of the store.

Walt. If you so much as touch me I'll have the law on you. You had your chancet and I'm as free as I ever was.

Thompson. Come on, John. I want to talk to you. Going home?

John. Yes. Has the woman gone up?

Thompson. Been gone for ten minutes. You'd better go on up yourself. I'll see if I can't fix this up for you and I'll be up later with Andy.

John. No. I aint goin to leave without fixin that young whelp there . . .

Walt. You lay a finger on me . . .

Thompson. Come on, John. You don't want a fight here. It wouldn't do you any good. The lad's right. Only get you into trouble. Come on. There's something I want to talk to you about.

Thompson leads John to the door with difficulty and goes outside with him.

Nosse *(admiringly).* You talked right up to him that time, Walt. Didn't he, Tom? Yes, sir. Have another cigar?

Walt. I knowed he aint got no hold on me and I aint afraid of him, neither. Lawyer Thompson knows it, too. He's a friend of old John's and he'd helped him if there'd been a way to do it. Wouldn't he?

Two of the boys. He sure would.

Nosse. He can't do anything to you, that's certain.

Barnood. But if you had a bit of decency in you you'd be willin to live up to your acts.

Thompson returns.

Walt. I don't have to and I aint goin to. Where's that cigar you was going to give me, Tad?

He goes over to the counter and gets another cigar while Thompson comes in and stands in front of the stove, his hands behind his back, his pose studied and severe.

Thompson. If I were you, Roche, I'd keep rather quiet about what I would do and what I wouldn't do.

There is a quality in his voice which makes Walt hold his lighted match until it burns his fingers. He does not light the cigar.

Walt. Why not? He's had me arrested and it aint done no good. He can't do a thing.

Thompson. That is just where you are very mistaken. He may have had you arrested but you've never been tried.

Walt. But old Sam Spenton . . .

Thompson. Is a justice of the peace and has just as much jurisdiction to try your case as Tad Nosse would have sitting on the top of that show case.

Walt *(nervously).* But these lads'll swear . . .

Thompson *(in the same monotonous, legal tone).* If you produced a regiment, it wouldn't necessarily make any difference. It would only mean that they were equally guilty. *(One of the three boys rises and makes his way as quietly as possible toward the door. Thompson wheels on the other two.)* Have you chaps sworn to anything?

One of them *(eagerly).* No, no, Mr. Thompson. We aint sworn to a thing.

Another. We didn't do it anyways. We just wanted to help Walt out'n a hole . . . We . . .

Another. No, Mr. Thompson, we . . .

Thompson. You're probably lying . . . but it doesn't matter. Now listen to me, Roche. If Serang ever takes this before a court of competent jurisdiction you could be sent down for twenty years.

Walt *(chokingly).* Twenty years?

The air seems to have grown close to everyone.

Thompson. Yes. Twenty years.

Walt. I . . . I . . . God! Twenty years. They couldn't do it.

Thompson. They could and after what you've said here to-day, they probably would.

Walt. What'll I do. Beat it?

Barnood. That wouldn't do you any good. They'd get you sooner or later.

Thompson. Serang asked my advice as a lawyer and I told him what I've told you but I don't like to see a lad of your age sent down for the best part of his life just because he's got a damn fool tongue in his head. You'd stand a very poor chance if this ever went to trial.

One by one the three boys slink out, very frightened, despicable figures.

Walt. What'll I do. Please, Mr. Thompson.

Thompson. You'd better see Serang as soon as you can. Perhaps he'll let you off if you'll marry her.

Walt. Where is he? Where did he go? I've got to catch him.

Thompson. He was going up home. You could catch him, if you ran.

Walt rushes to the door, followed by Tom, and goes out. The three men remain silent for an instant; Nosse behind the counter; Barnood and Thompson near the stove.

Barnood. Is that right, Mr. Thompson?

Thompson *(filling his pipe).* Well . . . it's a possibility.

Nosse. John ought to shot him, like I said.

Thompson *(infuriated).* By God, Nosse. I'd like to see you in that lad's shoes and hear how you'd talk then. Come on Andy.

Thompson and Barnood go toward the door.

Chronological List of Contents

The excerpts are listed according to the year of publication or first performance in English. Within a given year authors are listed alphabetically.

1886	Charles Mair	*Tecumseh*
1923	Merrill Denison	*Marsh Hay*
1936	Mazo de la Roche	*Whiteoaks*
1944	Lister Sinclair	*A Play on Words*
1946	Len Peterson	*Burlap Bags*
1947	Robertson Davies	*Overlaid*
1950	John Coulter	*Riel*
1955	Robertson Davies	*Hunting Stuart*
1960	James Reaney	*The Killdeer*
1962	W.O. Mitchell	*The Black Bonspiel of Wullie MacCrimmon*
1963	Charles Israel	*The Labyrinth*
1964	Don Owen	*Nobody Waved Goodbye*
1966	Norman Williams	*He Didn't Even Say Goodbye*
1967	John Coulter	*The Trial of Louis Riel*
	Gratien Gélinas	*Yesterday the Children Were Dancing*
	John Herbert	*Fortune and Men's Eyes*
	James Reaney	*Colours in the Dark*
	George Ryga	*The Ecstasy of Rita Joe*
	David Watmough	*Do You Remember One September Afternoon?*
1969	J.T. McDonough	*Charbonneau and Le Chef*
	Beverley Simons	*Crabdance*
	Sandy Stern	*Does Anybody Here Know Denny?*
	Jack Winter	*Party Day*
1970	David Freeman	*Creeps*
	William Fruet	*Goin' Down the Road*
1971	Thomas Hendry	*Fifteen Miles of Broken Glass*
	Harvey Markowitz	*Branch Plant*
1972	Roch Carrier	*La Guerre, Yes Sir!*
	David French	*Leaving Home*

Index of Scenes Classified According to Number and Sex of Characters

Some scenes appear under more than one heading when they are suitable for various uses.

One Character
1 Man — *La Guerre, Yes Sir!*
1 Woman — *The Killdeer*

Two Characters
2 Men — *Nobody Waved Goodbye*
2 Women — *The Killdeer*
The Labyrinth

Three Characters
3 Men — *Charbonneau and Le Chef*
Goin' Down the Road
Fifteen Miles of Broken Glass
Fortune and Men's Eyes
The Black Bonspiel of Wullie MacCrimmon
Whiteoaks
3 Women — *Do You Remember One September Afternoon?*
2 Men & 1 Woman — *Colours in the Dark*
Goin' Down the Road
Leaving Home
The Ecstasy of Rita Joe

Four Characters
4 Men — *Creeps*
3 Men & 1 Woman — *Branch Plant*
Grabdance
He Didn't Even Say Goodbye
Party Day
2 Men & 2 Women — *Tecumseh*
Yesterday the Children Were Dancing

Five Characters
5 Men — *Riel*
3 Men & 2 Women — *Overlaid*

Six Characters
6 Men — *The Trial of Louis Riel*

Seven Characters
6 Men & 1 Woman — *A Play on Words*
4 Men & 3 Women — *Does Anybody Here Know Denny?*

Eight Characters
8 Men — *Burlap Bags*
3 Men & 5 Women — *Hunting Stuart*

Nine Characters
9 Men — *Marsh Hay*

Crowd Scenes
Burlap Bags
Colours in the Dark
Goin' Down the Road
La Guerre, Yes Sir!
Riel
Tecumseh
The Ecstasy of Rita Joe
The Trial of Louis Riel

A Selected List of Theatre Companies in Canada

Victoria	Bastion Theatre Victoria Fair
Vancouver	Savage God Playhouse Theatre Company
Calgary	Theatre Calgary
Edmonton	Theatre 3 Citadel
Regina	Globe Theatre
Winnipeg	Manitoba Theatre Centre Rainbow Stage
Stratford	Stratford Festival
Niagara-On-The-Lake	Shaw Festival
Toronto	Canadian Mime Theatre Factory Lab Theatre Passe-Muraille Canadian Puppet Festivals Toronto Workshop Productions St. Lawrence Centre Fondation "Touring Players" Foundation Studio Lab Young People's Theatre
Ottawa	National Arts Centre
Montreal	Théâtre de Marjoliane Théâtre d'aujourd'hui Revue Theatre Le Trident Théâtre de Quat'sous Théâtre populaire du Quebec Théâtre du Nouveau Monde Théâtre du Rideau Vert Théâtre International de Montreal Centaur Theatre Saidye Bronfman
Fredericton	Theatre New Brunswick
Charlottetown	Charlottetown Festival
Halifax	Neptune Theatre
St. John's	Newfoundland Arts & Culture Centre

Bibliography

An asterisk denotes a work from which an excerpt has been taken for use in this Scenebook.

Plays.

- Alianuk, Hrant. *Tantrume*. Toronto: Playwrights Co-op, 1972.
- Bolt, Carol. *Buffalo Jump*. Toronto: Playwrights Co-op, 1972.
- Borsook, Henry. *Three Weedings of a Hunchback*, in *Canadian Plays from Hart House*, I. Ed. V. Massey. Toronto: Macmillan, 1926.*
- Burgess, Ivan. *Horseshoe House*. Toronto: Playwrights Co-op, 1972.
- Campbell, William. *Poetical Tragedies*. Toronto: William Briggs, 1908.
- Gapson, Louis. *The True North Blueprint: A Trilogy*. Toronto: Playwrights Co-op, 1972.
- Carrier, Roch. *La Guerre, Yes Sir!* Trans. Suzanne Grossman, 1972. Unpublished script.*
- Cohen, M. Charles. *The Member from Trois-Rivières: A One-Act Play Based on the Life of Ezekial Hart*. Montreal: Canadian Jewish Congress, 1959.
- Coulter, John. *Riel: a Play in Two Parts*. Toronto: Ryerson, 1962.*
- _____.*The Trial of Louis Riel*. Ottawa: Oberon, 1968.*
- Davies, Robertson. *Overlaid*. Toronto: Samuel French, 1948.* *Eros at Breakfast and Other Plays*. Introduction by Tyrone Guthrie. Toronto: Clarke, Irwin, 1949.
- _____.*Fortune My Foe*. Toronto: Clarke, Irwin, 1949.
- _____.*A Masque of Aesop*. Toronto: Clarke, Irwin, 1952.
- _____.*A Masque of Mr. Punch*. Toronto: Ozdoes University Press, 1963.
- _____.*Four Favourite Plays*. Toronto: Clarke, Irwin, 1968.
- _____.*Hunting Stuart*, in *Hunting Stuart and Other Plays*. Toronto: New Press, 1972.
- Davis, Rae. *Five Fugues For Isaac Newton*. Toronto: Playwrights Co-op, 1972.
- de la Roche, Mazo. *Whiteoaks: a Play*. Boston: Little, Brown Co., 1940.*
- Denison, Merrill. *Marsh Hay*, in *The Unheroic North: Four Canadian Plays.* Toronto: McClelland and Stewart, 1923.
- Freeman, David. *Creeps*. Toronto: University of Toronto Press, 1972.*
- _____.*Battering Ram*. Toronto: Playwrights Co-op, 1972.
- French, David. *Leaving Home*. Toronto: New Press 1972.*
- Fruet, William. *Goin' Down the Road*. Unpublished film script.*
- Gélinas, Gratien. *Bousille and the Just*. Trans. Kenneth Johnson. Toronto: Clarke, Irwin, 1961.
- _____.*Tit-Coq*. Toronto: Clarke, Irwin, 1966.
- _____.*Yesterday the Children Were Dancing*. Trans. Mavor Moore. Toronto: Clarke, Irwin, 1967.*
- Gurik, Robert. *The Hanged Man*. Trans. Philip London and Laurence
- Bérard. Introduction by Philip London. Toronto: new press, 1972.
- Hardin, Herschel. *Esker Mike and his Wife Agıluk*. In *The Drama Review*, vol. 14, no. 1 (Fall, 1969).

- Heavysege, Charles. *Saul: a Drama, in Three Parts.* Boston: Fields, Osgood Co., 1869.
- Hendry, Thomas. *Fifteen Miles of Broken Glass.* Toronto: Playwrights Co-op, 1972.*
- Henry, Ann. *Lulu Street.* Toronto: Playwrights Co-op, 1972.
- Herbert, John. *Fortune and Men's Eyes.* New York: Grove Press, 1967.*
- Israel, Charles. *The Labyrinth.* Toronto: Macmillan, 1969.*
- Johnson, Chris. *Trips.* Toronto: Playwrights Co-op, 1972.
- Joudry, Patricia. *Teach Me How To Cry.* New York: Dramatists Play Service, 1955.
- Koch, Eric and Tovell, Vincent. *Success of a Mission: Lord Durham in Canada; a Play for Television.* With J. T. Saywell, historical adviser. Toronto: Clarke, Irwin, 1961.
- Mair, Charles. *Tecumseh: A Drama,* in *Tecumseh and Canadian Poems. Master Works of Canadian Authors* vol. XIV. Ed. John Garvin. Toronto: Radisson Society of Canada, 1926.*
- Markowitz, Harvey. *Branch Plant.* Toronto: Playwrights Co-op, 1972.*
- McConnell, Peter. *The Cool Constable or More About Moses in a Minute.* Toronto: Playwrights Co-op, 1972.
- McDonough, John Thomas. *Charbonneau and Le Chef.* McClelland and Stewart, 1968.*
- *Mictchell, W. O. *The Black Bonspiel of Wullie MacCrimmon,* in *Three Worlds of Drama.* Ed. J. Livesley. Toronto: Macmillan, 1966.
- Owen, Don. *Nobody Waved Goodbye,* in *Nobody Waved Goodbye and Other Plays.* Ed. H. Voaden. Toronto: Macmillan, 1966.
- Palmer, John. *Bland Hysteria: A Farce in Two Acts.* Toronto: Playwrights Co-op, 1972.
- _____.*A Touch of God in the Golden Age.* Toronto: Playwrights Co-op, 1972.
- Peterson, Len. *The Great Hunger.* Agincourt, Ontario: Book Society, 1967.
- _____.*Burlap Bags.* Toronto: Playwrights Co-op, 1972.*
- _____.*Women in the Attic.* Toronto: Playwrights Co-op, 1972.
- Reaney, James. *The Killdeer and Other Plays.* Toronto: Macmillan, 1962.
- _____.*Colours in the Dark.* Vancouver and Toronto: Talonplays with Macmillan, 1969.*
- Reeves, John Michael. *A Beach of Strangers.* Toronto: Oxford University Press, 1961.
- Ringwood, Gwen Pharis. *Still Stands the House.* Toronto: Samuel French, 1939.
- _____.*Lament for Harmonica.* Ottawa: Ottawa Little Theatre Workshop, Set 1 no. 10, 1960.
- Ryga, George. *The Ecstasy of Rita Joe and Other Plays.* Ed. Brian Parker. Toronto: new press, 1971.
- _____.*Captives of the Faceless Drummer.* Vancouver: Talonbooks, 1971.
- Simons, Beverley. *Crabdance.* Vancouver: Talonbooks, 1972.*
- *Sinclair, Lister. *A Play on Words,* in *A Play on Words and Other Radio Plays.* Toronto and Vancouver: Dent, 1948.
- _____.*Socrates.* Agincourt, Ontario: Book Society, 1957.
- Stern, sandy. *Does Anybody Here Know Denny?* in *The Demanding Age: An Anthology of assorted Contemporary Literature.* Ed. Ronald Side and Ralph Greenfield. Toronto: McGraw-Hill, 1970.*

- Walker, George. *Ambush at Tether's End.* Toronto: Playwrights Co-op, 1972.
- *Watmough, David. *Do You Remember One September Afternoon?* in *Names For the Numbered Years; Three Plays.* Vancouver: Bau-XI Gallery, 1967.
- Williams, Norman. *He Didn't Even Say Goodbye.* Toronto: Playwrights Co-op, 1972.*
- Winter, Jack. *Party Day.* Toronto: Playwrights Co-op, 1972.

ANTHOLOGIES:

- Alive Theatre Workshop, ed. *Dialogue and Dialectic: A Canadian Anthology of Short Plays.* Guelph, Ontario: Alive Press Ltd., n.d. (1973).
- Benson, Eugene. *Encounter: Canadian Drama in Four Media.* Toronto: Methuen, 1973.
- Moore, Mavor, ed. *Four Canadian Playwrights* Toronto: Holt, Rinehart & Winston, 1973.
- Canadian Authors' Association *One Act Plays by Canadian Authors: Nineteen Short Canadian Plays.* Montreal: Canadian Authors' Association, 1926.
- Richards, Stanley, ed. *Canada On Stage: A Collection of One-Act Plays.* Toronto: Clarke, Irwin, 1960.
- Massey, Vincent, ed. *Canadian Plays From Hart House Theatre.* 2 vols. Toronto: Macmillan, 1926-7.
- Voaden Herman A., ed. *Six Canadian Plays.* Toronto: Copp Clark, 1930.

BIBLIOGRAPHIES

- Ball, John L., ed. "Theatre in Canada: a Bibliography". *Canadian Literature,* no. 14 (Autumn 1962), 85-100.
- *The Brock Bibliography of Published Canadian Stage-Plays in English, 1900-1972.* Brock University Department of Drama. Toronto: Playwrights Co-op, 1972.
- Canadian Association for Adult Education. *Selective Bibliography of Canadian Drama.* Canadian Association for Adult Education, 1957.

CATALOGUES

- Milne, William Samuel, ed. *Canadian Full-Length Plays in English: a*
- *Preliminary Annotated Catologue,* 2 parts. Ottawa: Dominion Drama Festival, 1964-66.
- *Canadian Plays.* Toronto: Playwrights Co-op, Summer, 1972.
- *100 Canadian Plays.* Toronto: Playwrights Co-op, Winter, 1973.

OTHER USEFUL REFERENCES

- New, William H., ed. *Dramatists in Canada: Selected Essays.* Vancouver: University of British Columbia Press, 1972.
- Edwards, Murray D. *A Stage in Our Past: English Language Theatre in*
- *Eastern Canada from the 1790's to 1914.* Toronto: University of Toronto Press, 1968.
- Lee, Alvin A. *James Reaney.* New York: Twayne, 1968.

- *The Awkward Stage: The Ontario Theatre Study Report.* Toronto: Methuen, 1969.
- McIntosh, James C., ed. *The Performing Arts in Canada.* Published quarterly by the Performing Arts in Canada Publishing Co. Ltd., P.O. Box 517, Postal Station "F", Toronto 5.
- *The Stage in Canada: a Monthly Magazine on Theatre, Opera and Dance.* Published by Canadian Theatre Centre, 280, Bloor Street West, Toronto 5.
- *Theatre Yearbook.* A publication of Canadian Theatre Centre.
- Watters, Reginald E. *A Check List of Canadian Literature, 1628-1950.* Toronto: University of Toronto Press, 1972.

Acknowledgments

Canadian Speakers' and Writers' Services, for *A Play on Words*, by Lister Sinclair.
Clarke, Irwin and Company, Limited, for *Yesterday the Children Were Dancing*, by Gratien Gélinas.
Editions du Jour, Inc., for *La Guerre, Yes Sir!*, by Roch Carrier.
Samuel French (Canada) Ltd., for *Overlaid*, by Robertson Davies.
Grove Press, Inc., for *Fortune and Men's Eyes*, by John Herbert (©1967 John Herbert).
Charles Israel, for *The Labyrinth*, by Charles Israel.
The Macmillan Co. of Canada, Ltd., and The National Film Board of Canada, for *Nobody Waved Goodbye*, by Don Owen.
McClelland and Stewart, Ltd., for *Marsh Hay*, by Merrill Denison, *Charbonneau and Le Chef*, by J. T. McDonough.
McGraw-Hill Ryerson, Limited, for *Riel*, by John Coulter.
W. O. Mitchell, for *The Black Bonspiel of Wullie MacCrimmon* from *Three Worlds of Drama* (Macmillan, 1966).
New Press, Educational Division, and The Macmillan Co. of Canada, Ltd., for *Hunting Stuart*, by Robertson Davies, *Leaving Home*, by David French, *The Killdeer*, by James Reaney.
Oberon Press, for *The Trial of Louis Riel*, by John Coulter.
Renee Paris, for *The Ecstasy of Rita Joe*, by George Ryga, and *Crabdance*, by Beverley Simons.
Len Peterson, for *Burlap Bags*, by Len Peterson.
Playwrights' Co-op, for *Fifteen Miles of Broken Glass*, by Tom Hendry, and *Branch Plant*, by Harvey Markowitz.
Don Shebib, for *Goin' Down the Road*, by Don Shebib.
Dr. Sandy G. Stern, for *Does Anybody Here Know Denny?*
Talon Books, The Macmillan Co. of Canada, Ltd. and Sybil Hutchinson, for *Colours in the Dark*, by James Reaney.
University of Toronto Press, for *Creeps*, by David Freeman.
David Watmough, for *Do You Remember One September Afternoon?*
Norman Williams, for *He Didn't Even Say Goodbye*, by Norman Williams.
Jack Winter, for *Party Day*, by Jack Winter.

Every care has been taken to acknowledge copyright owners correctly. The editor and publisher would welcome information that will permit the correction of any errors or omissions in subsequent printings.

ANDREW PARKIN is Professor of English at the University of British Columbia. Born and educated in England, he taught in both England and Hong Kong before coming to Canada. He has a wide interest in the dramatic arts and is currently collaborating in translating from Russian a book on *King Lear* by the renowned Soviet film director, Kozintsev.

JOHN STEVENS, General Editor of Festival Editions, is Professor of English in the Faculty of Education, University of Toronto. He has had a widely varied career in education and is author or co-author of numerous books used in Canadian schools and colleges.